BIG-NOTE PIANO

TODAY'S POP HITS

3RD EDITION

contents

ISBN 978-1-4950-6496-8

HAL•LEONARD®
CORPORATION
7777 W. BLUEMOUND RD. P.O. BOX 13819 MILWAUKEE, WI 53213

Visit Hal Leonard Online at
www.halleonard.com

ALL OF ME

Words and Music by JOHN STEPHENS
and TOBY GAD

Moderately, with feeling

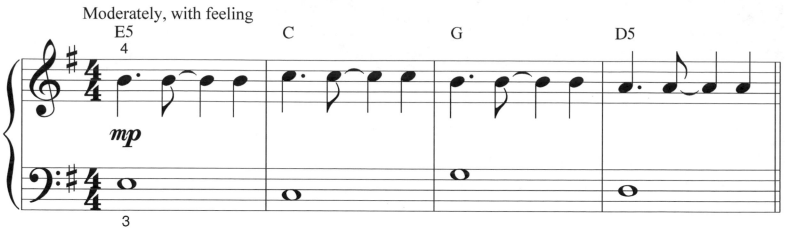

What would I do with-out your smart mouth draw-in' me
How man-y times do I have to tell you, e-ven when you're

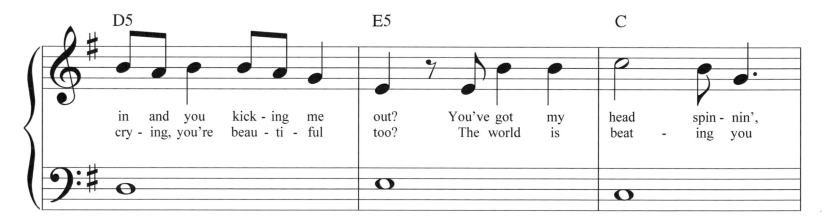

in and you kick-ing me out? You've got my head spin-nin',
cry-ing, you're beau-ti-ful too? The world is beat-ing you

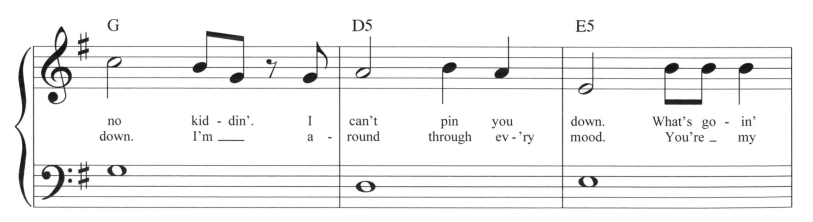

no kid-din'. I can't pin you down. What's go-in'
down. I'm ____ a-round through ev-'ry mood. You're ___ my

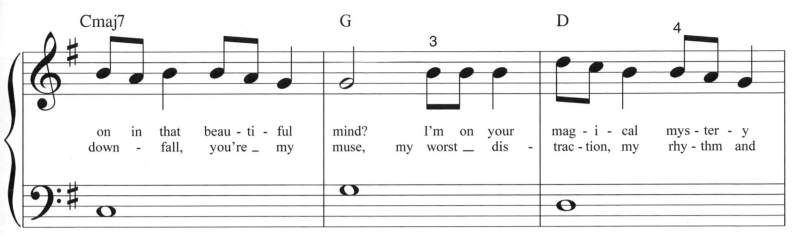

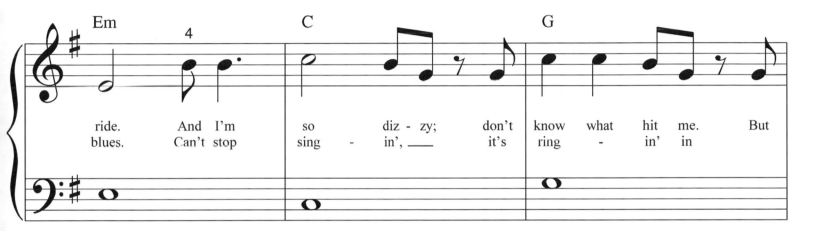

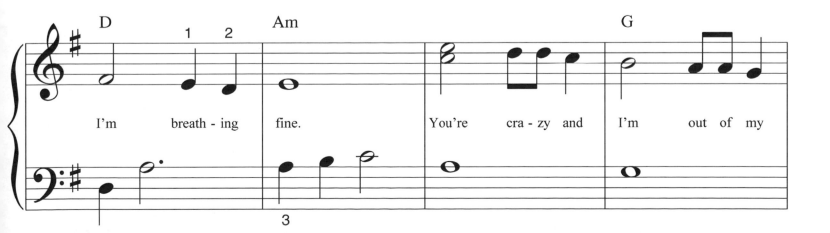

4

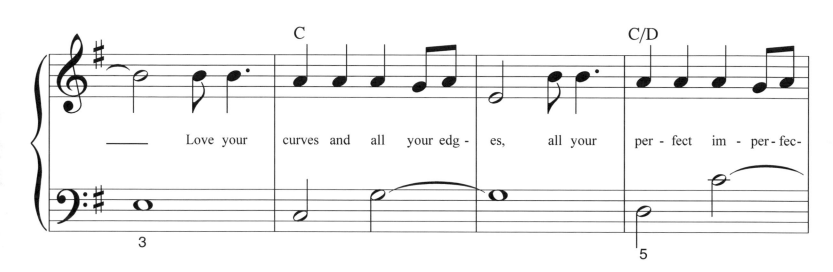

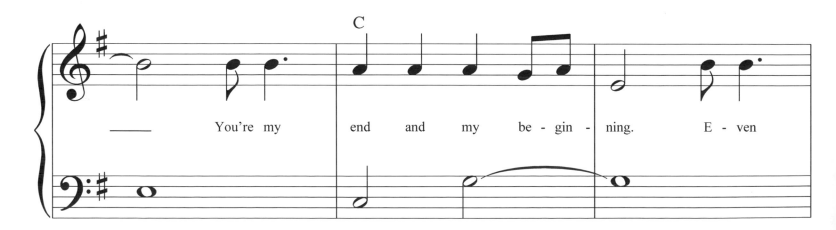

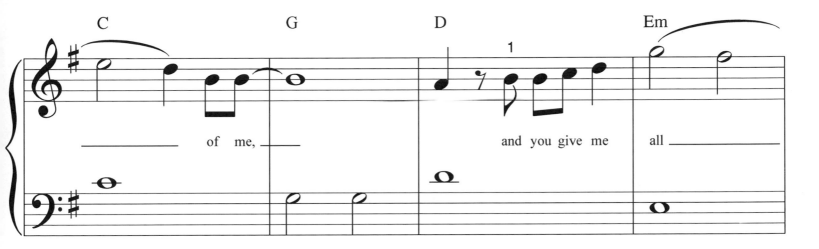

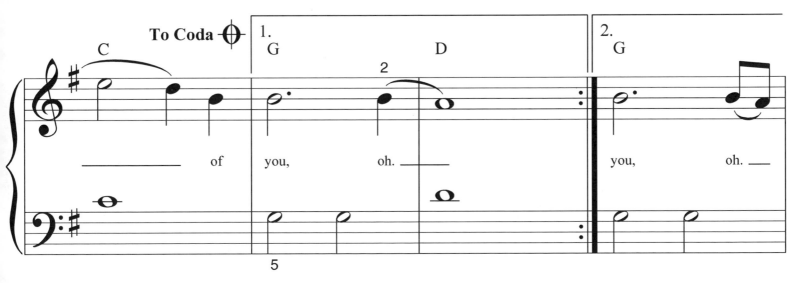

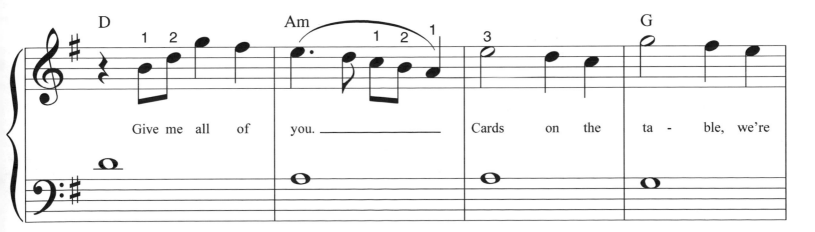

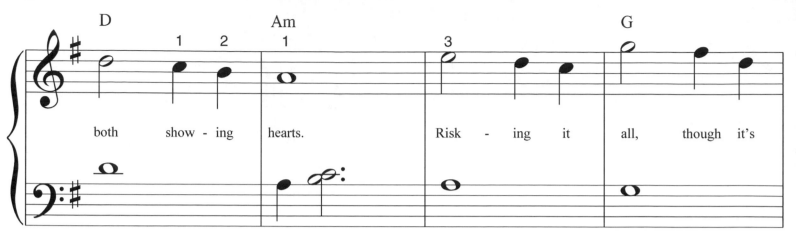

both show - ing hearts. Risk - ing it all, though it's

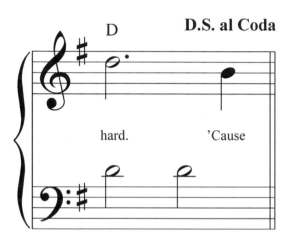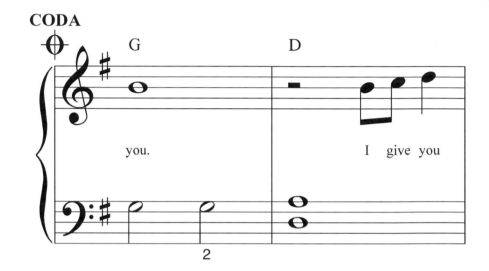

hard. 'Cause

D.S. al Coda

CODA

you. I give you

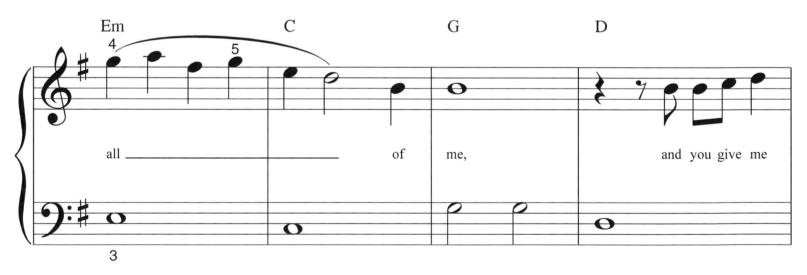

all _____ of me, and you give me

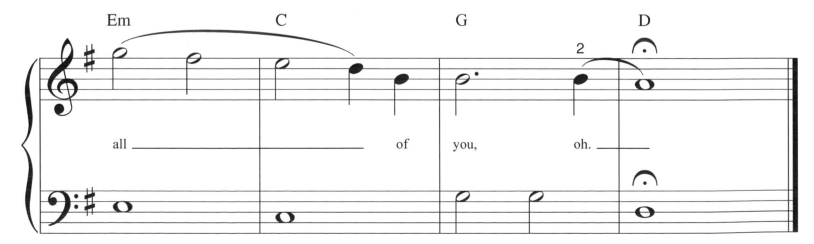

all _____ of you, oh. _____

GRENADE

Words and Music by BRUNO MARS,
ARI LEVINE, PHILIP LAWRENCE,
BRODY BROWN, CLAUDE KELLY
and ANDREW WYATT

Moderately fast

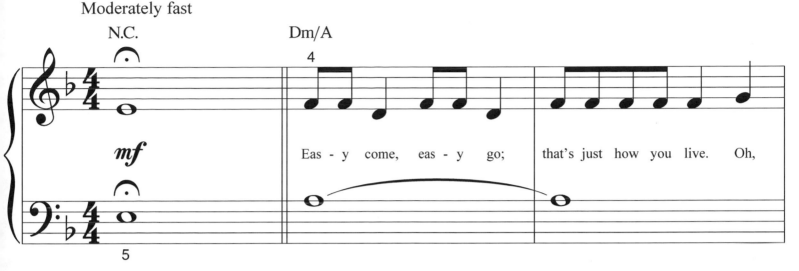

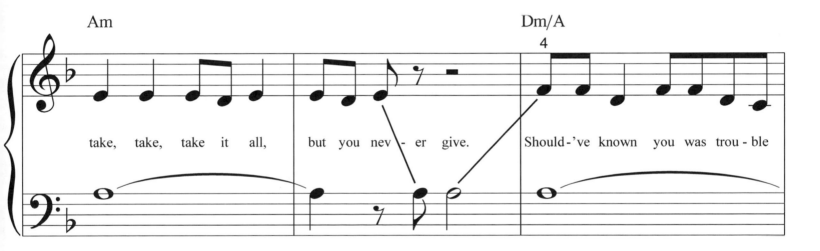

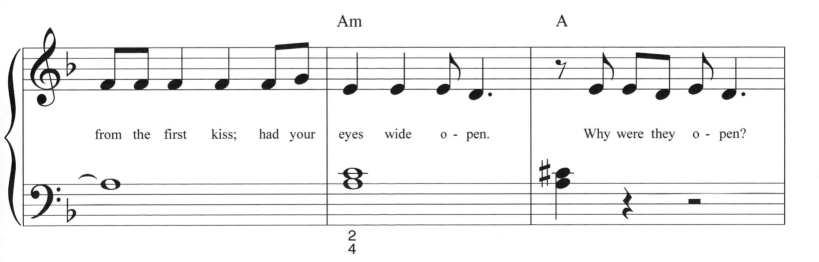

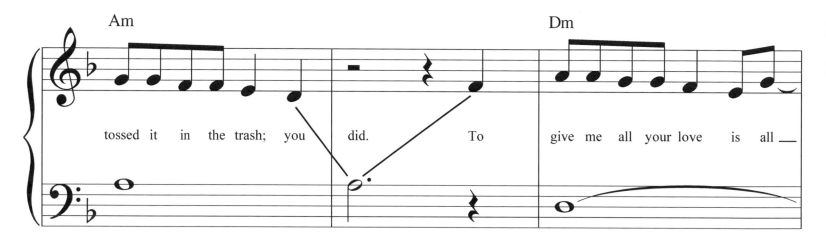

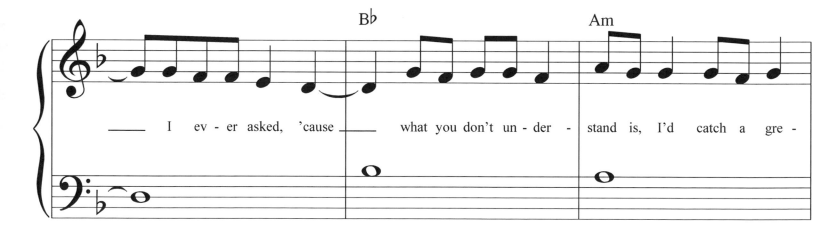

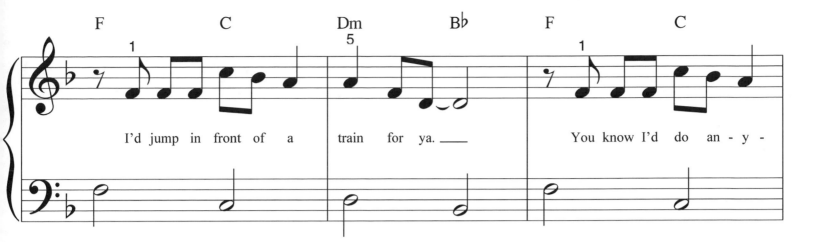

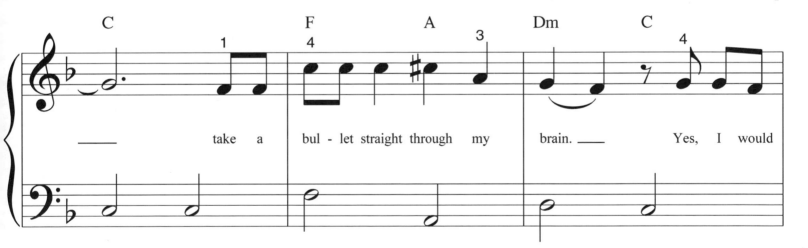

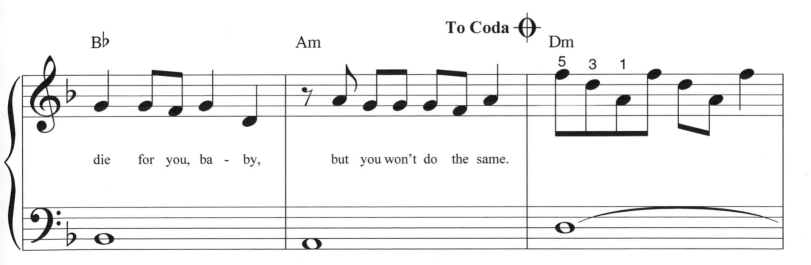

10

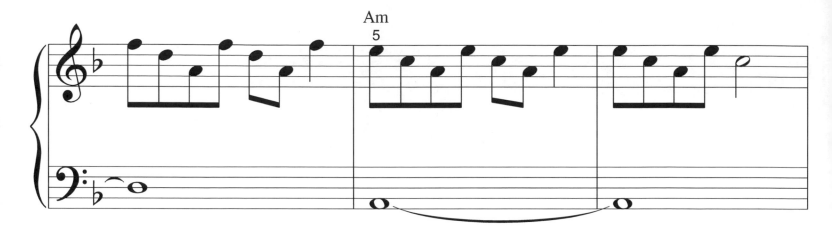

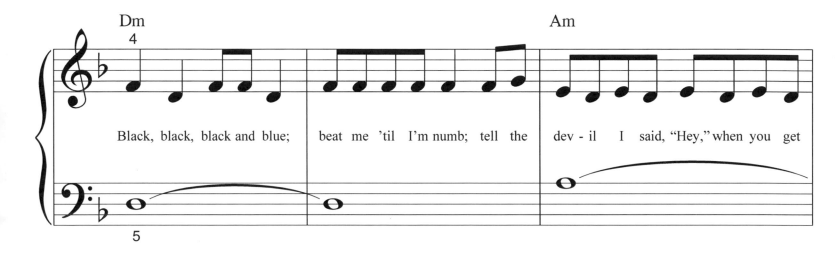

Black, black, black and blue; beat me 'til I'm numb; tell the dev - il I said, "Hey," when you get

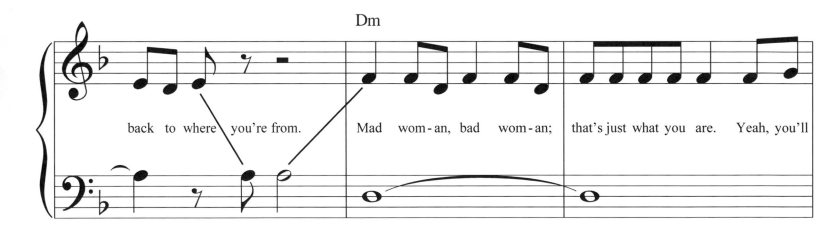

back to where you're from. Mad wom-an, bad wom-an; that's just what you are. Yeah, you'll

D.S. al Coda

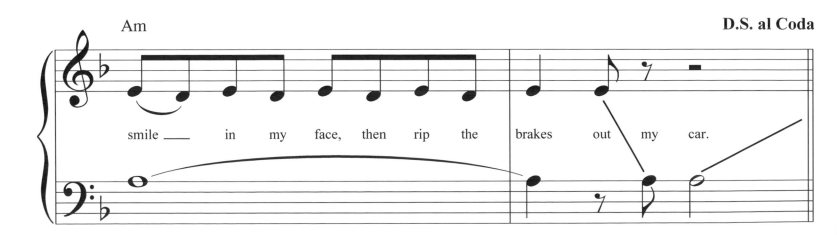

smile ____ in my face, then rip the brakes out my car.

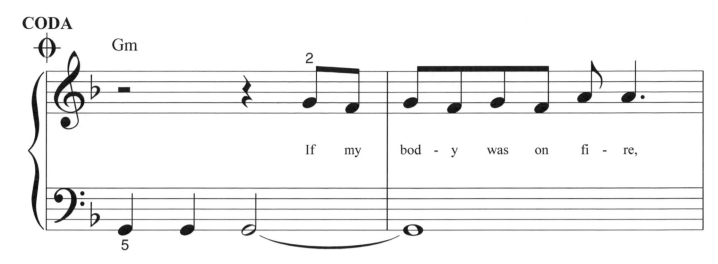

CODA

Gm

If my bod-y was on fi-re,

Dm   Gm

ooh, you'd watch me burn down in flames.   You said you

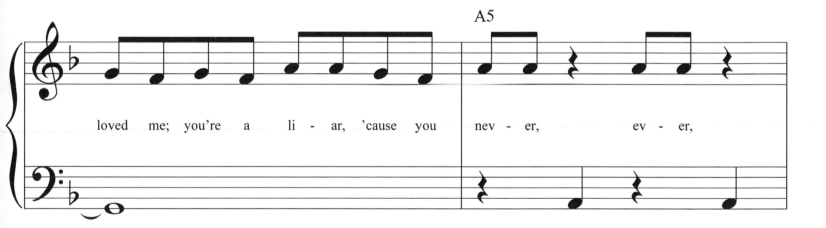

A5

loved me; you're a li-ar, 'cause you   nev-er,   ev-er,

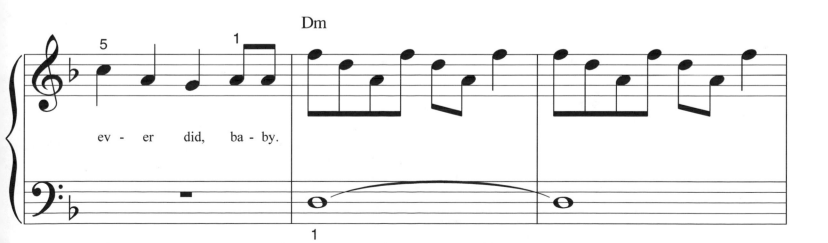

Dm

ev-er did, ba-by.

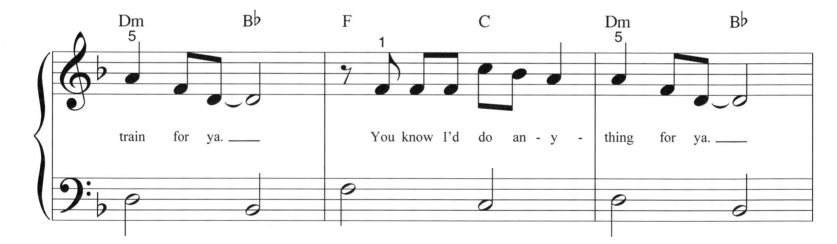

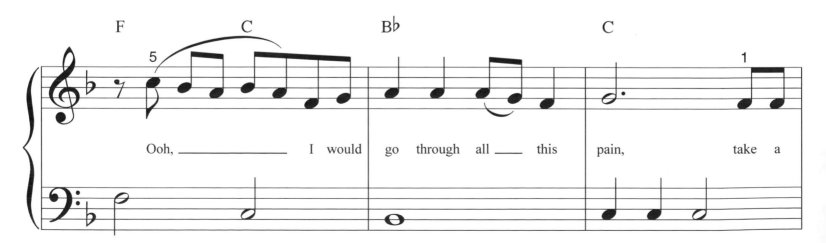

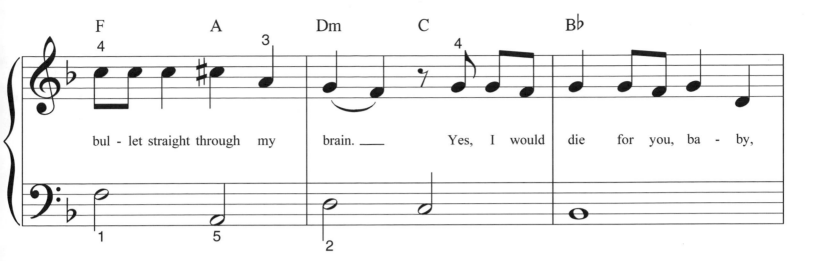

bul - let straight through my brain. ___ Yes, I would die for you, ba - by,

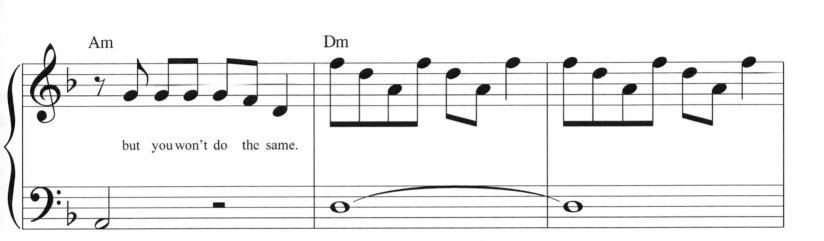

but you won't do the same.

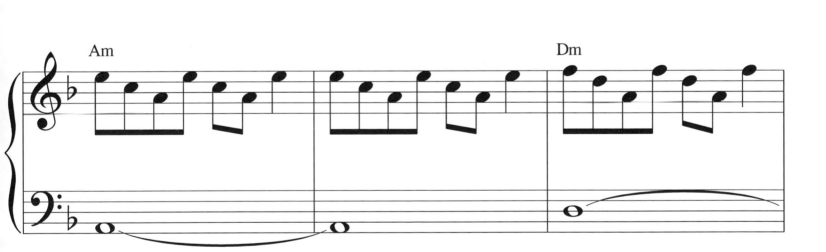

HAPPY
from DESPICABLE ME 2

Words and Music by
PHARRELL WILLIAMS

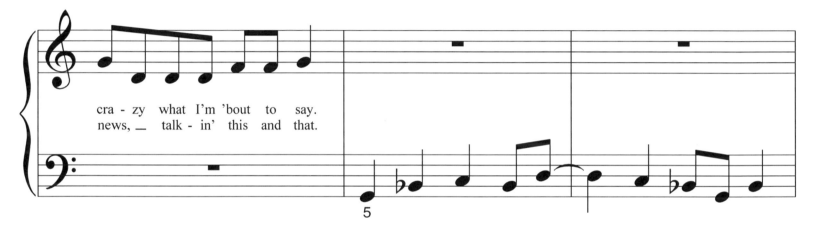

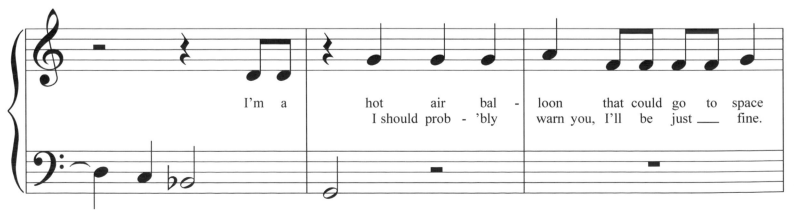

with the air like I don't
No of-fense to

care, ba - by, by the way. _____
you, don't _____ waste your time. _____

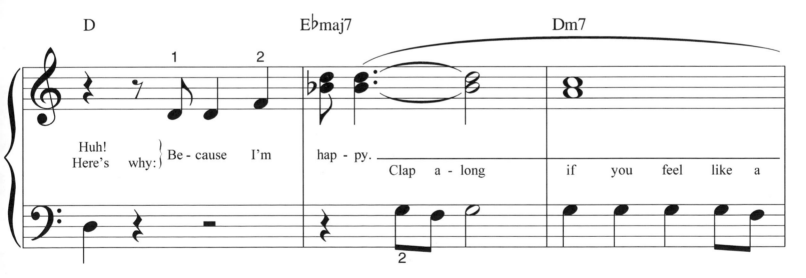

D   E♭maj7   Dm7

Huh!
Here's why: } Be - cause I'm hap - py. _____
Clap a - long if you feel like a

G   N.C.   E♭maj7

room with - out a roof.   Be - cause I'm hap - py. _____
Clap a - long

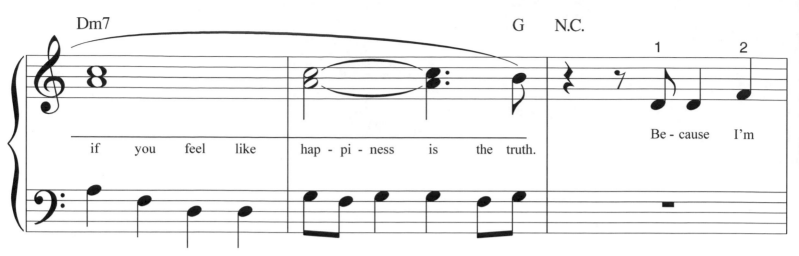

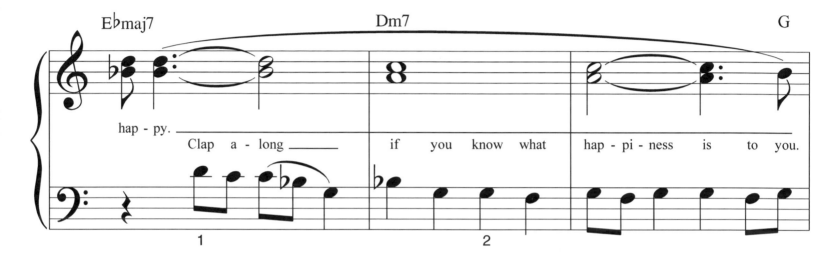

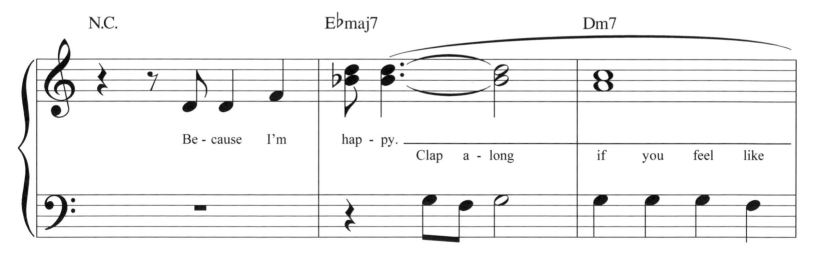

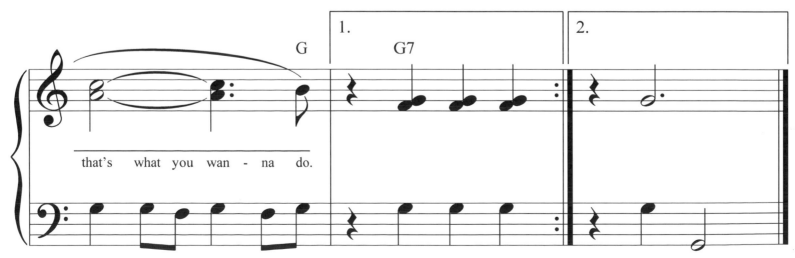

HELLO

Words and Music by ADELE ADKINS
and GREG KURSTIN

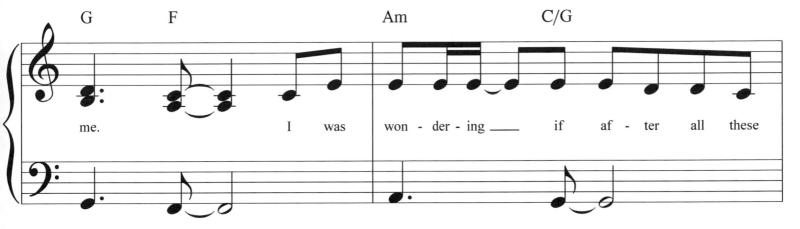

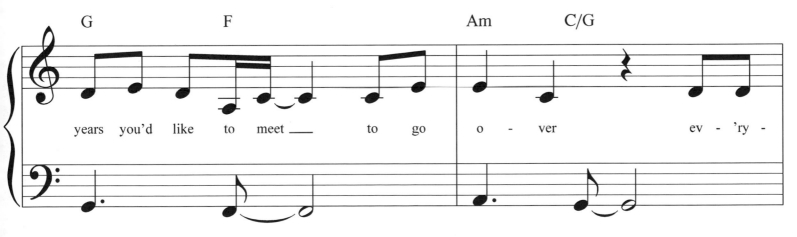

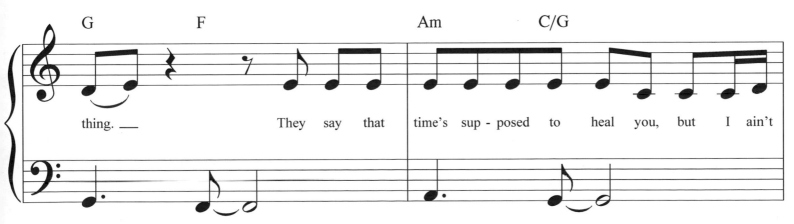

18

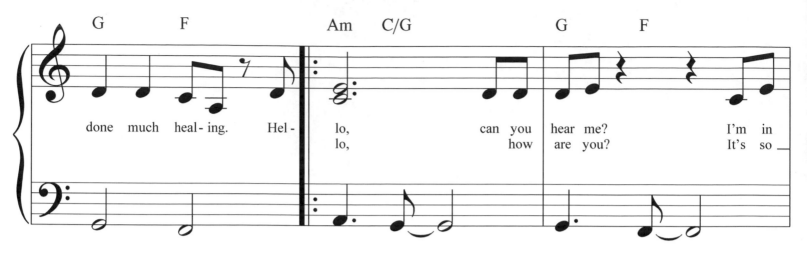

G   F   Am   C/G   G   F

done much heal - ing. Hel - | lo,   can you hear me?   I'm in
                            lo,   how   are you?   It's so

Am   C/G   G   F

Cal - i - for - nia, dream - ing a - bout | who we used to be _____ when we were
typ - i - cal _____ of me to talk a - | bout my - self; I'm sor - ry. _____ I

Am   C/G   G   F

young - er   and   free. _____   I've   for -
hope _____   that you're well. _____   Did   you

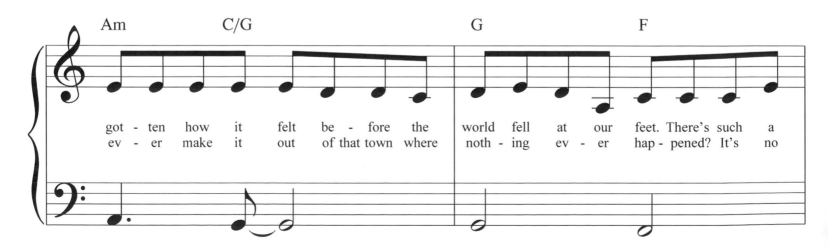

Am   C/G   G   F

got - ten how it felt be - fore the | world fell at our feet. There's such a
ev - er make it out of that town where | noth - ing ev - er hap - pened? It's no

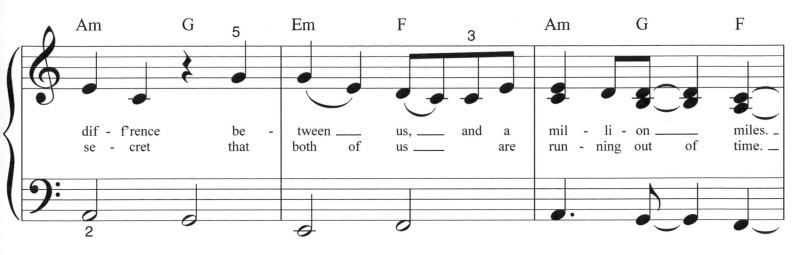

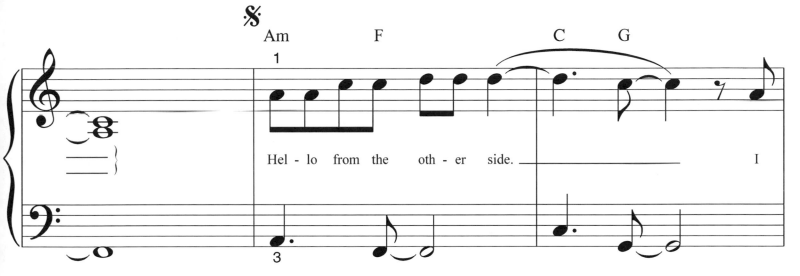

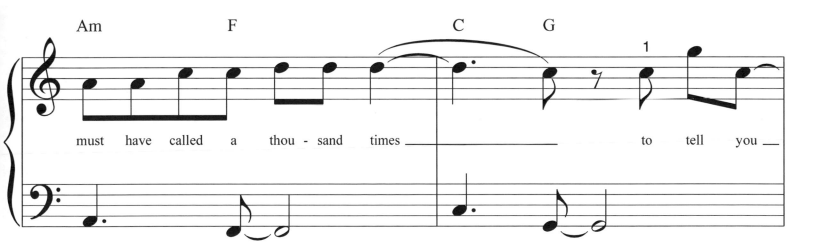

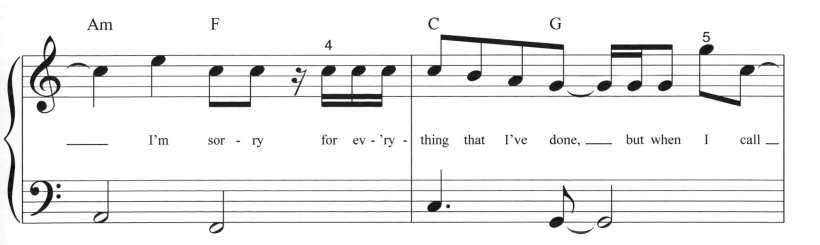

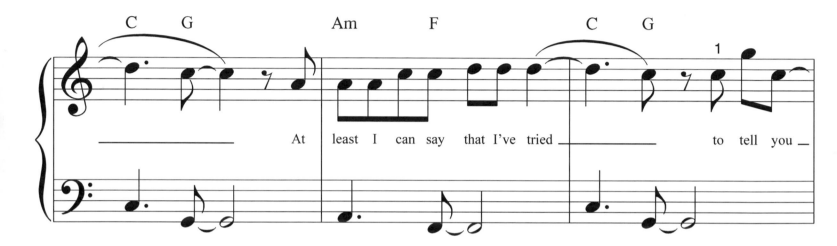

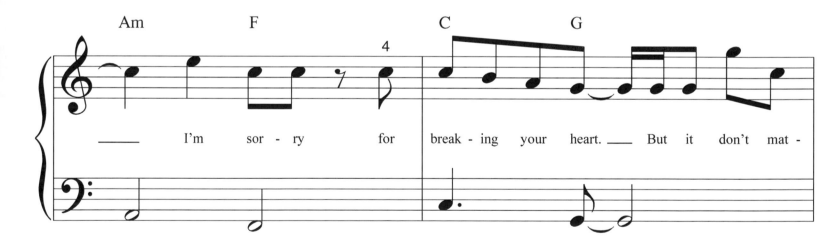

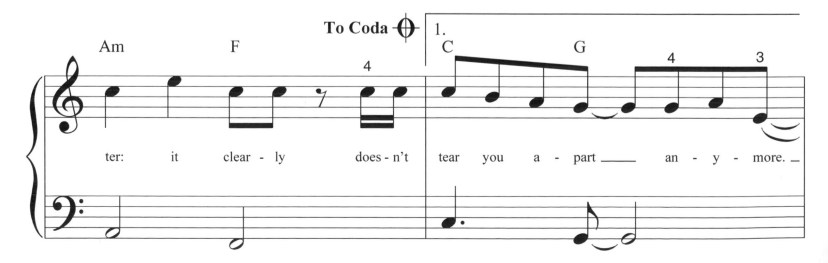

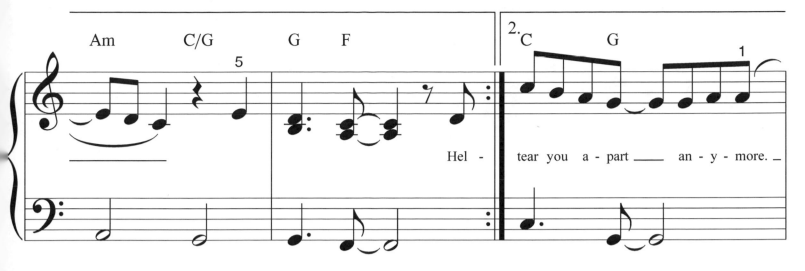

Am   C/G   G   F   2. C   G

Hel -   tear you a - part ____ an - y - more.

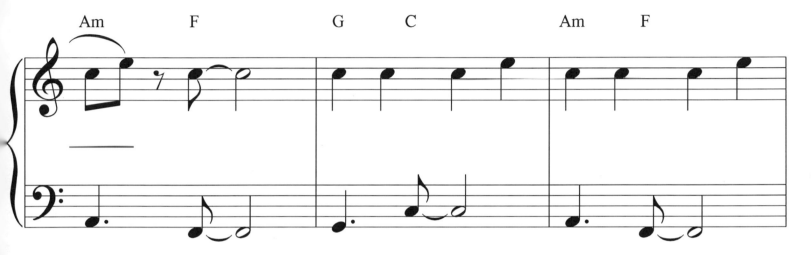

Am   F   G   C   Am   F

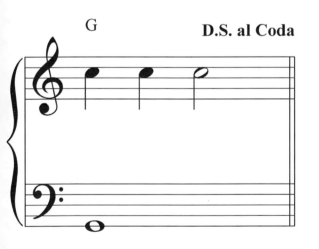

G   **D.S. al Coda**

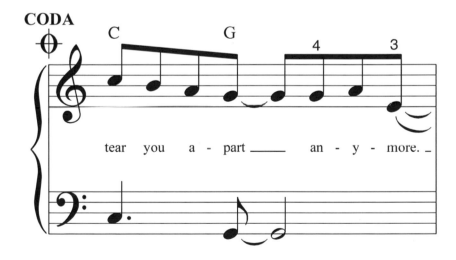

CODA   C   G

tear you a - part ____ an - y - more.

Am   C/G   G   F   Am

JUST GIVE ME A REASON

Words and Music by ALECIA MOORE,
JEFF BHASKER and NATE RUESS

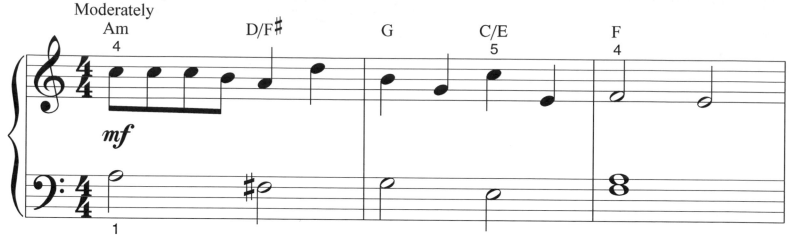

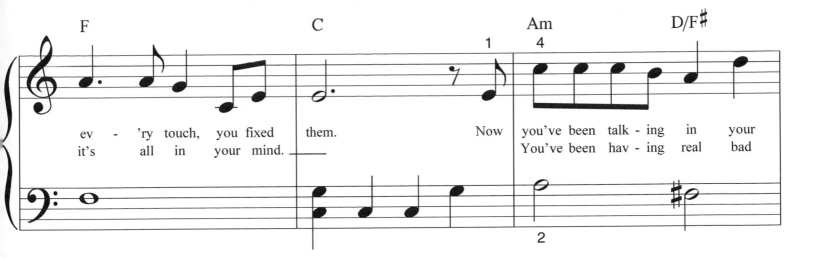

ev - 'ry touch, you fixed them. Now you've been talk - ing in your
it's all in your mind. You've been hav - ing real bad

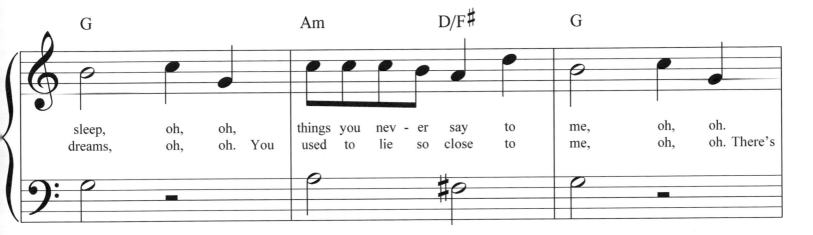

sleep, oh, oh, things you nev - er say to me, oh, oh.
dreams, oh, oh. You used to lie so close to me, oh, oh. There's

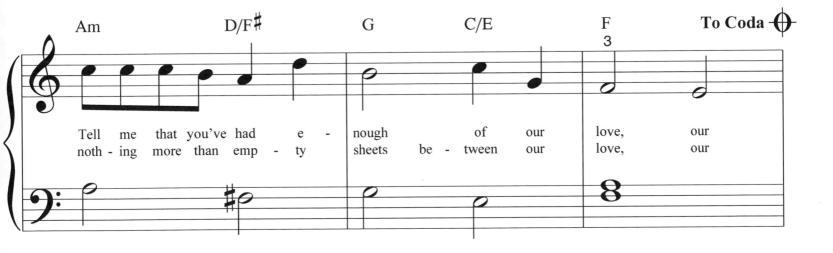

Tell me that you've had e - nough of our love, our
noth - ing more than emp - ty sheets be - tween our love, our

To Coda ⊕

love.
Just give me a rea - son, just a lit - tle bit's e - nough, just a

sec - ond. We're not bro-ken, just bent, ____ and we can learn to love a - gain. ____ It's in the stars. It's been

writ-ten in the scars on our hearts: we're not bro-ken, just bent, ____ and we can learn to love a - gain. ___

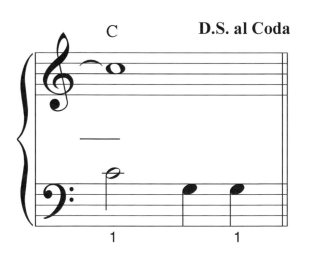

D.S. al Coda

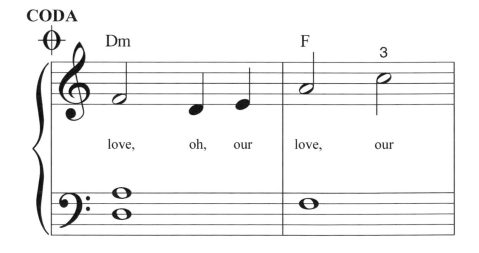

CODA

love, oh, our love, our

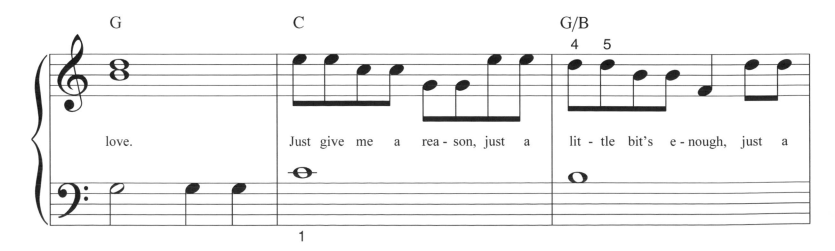

love. Just give me a rea - son, just a lit - tle bit's e - nough, just a

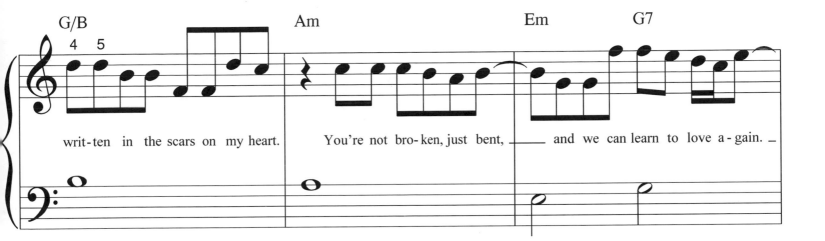

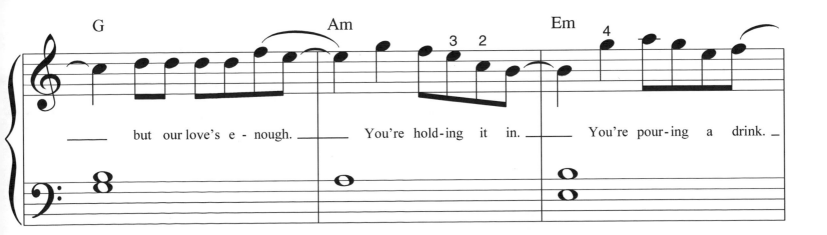

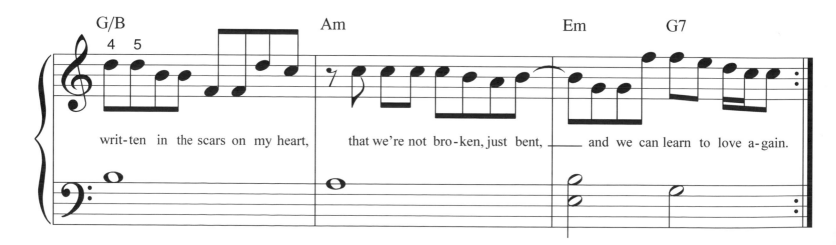

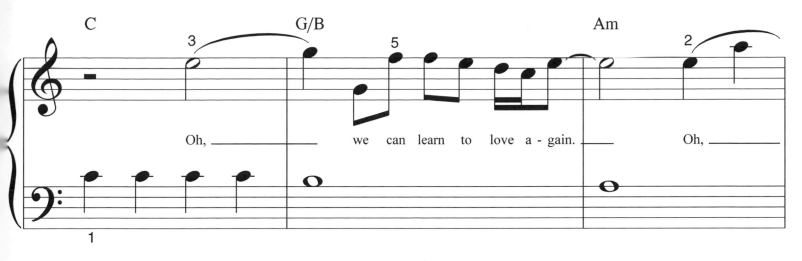

Oh, _____ we can learn to love a - gain. _____ Oh, _____

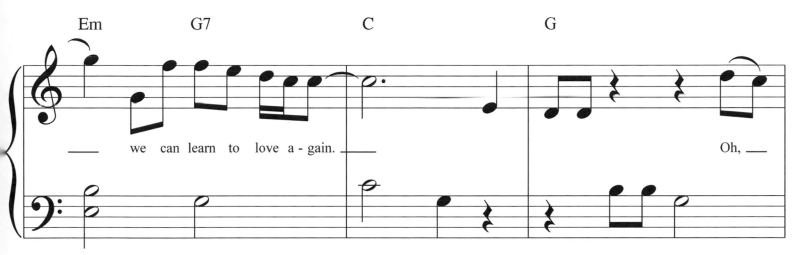

_____ we can learn to love a - gain. _____ Oh, ___

that we're not bro - ken, just bent, _____ and we can learn to love a - gain. ___

rit.

STAY

Words and Music by MIKKY EKKO
and JUSTIN PARKER

Moderate Ballad

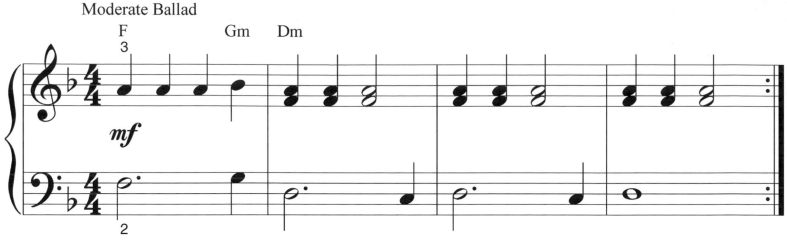

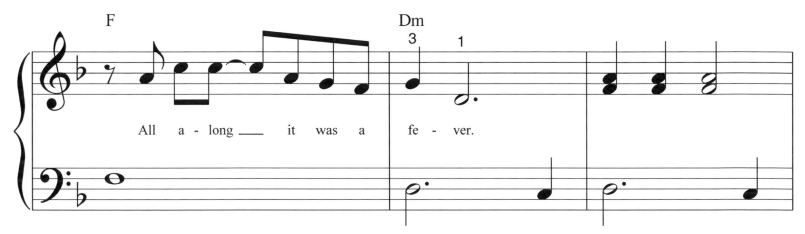

All a-long ___ it was a fe - ver.

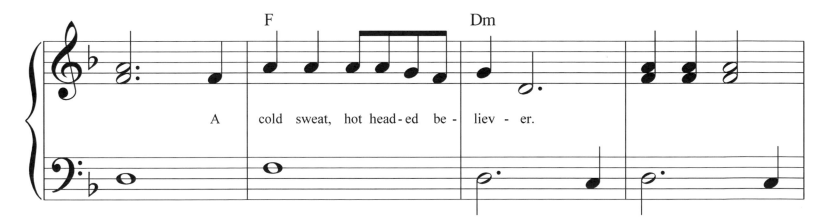

A cold sweat, hot head-ed be - liev - er.

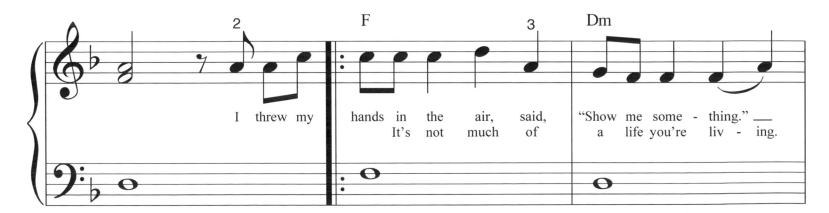

I threw my hands in the air, said,
It's not much of

"Show me some - thing." ___
a life you're liv - ing.

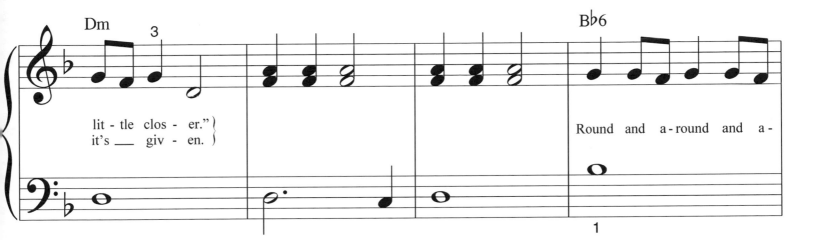

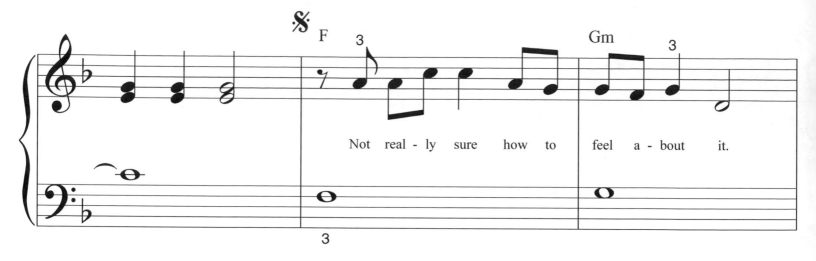

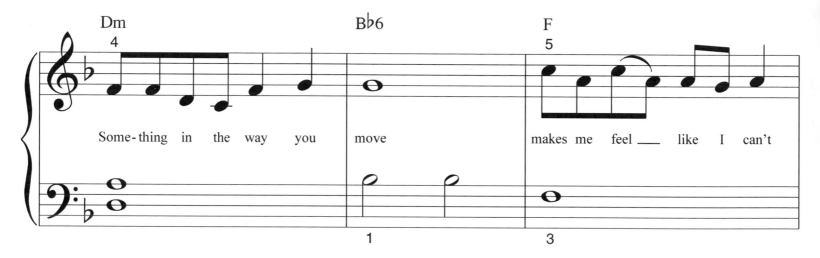

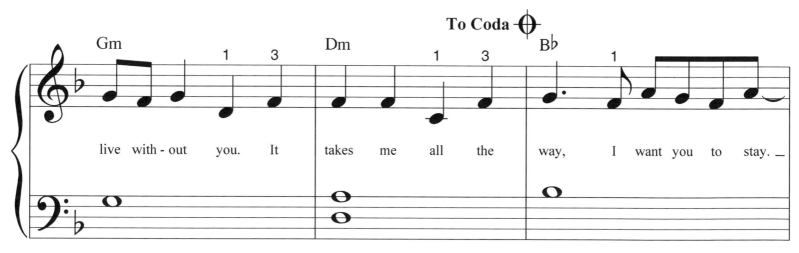

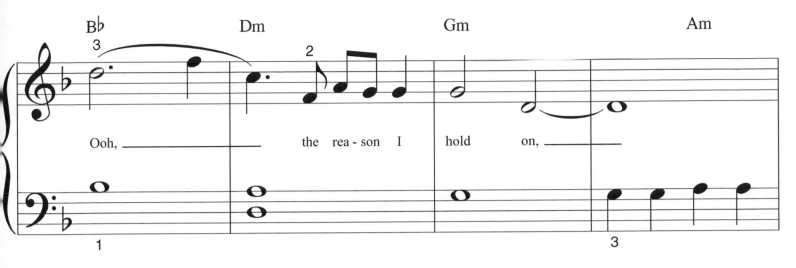

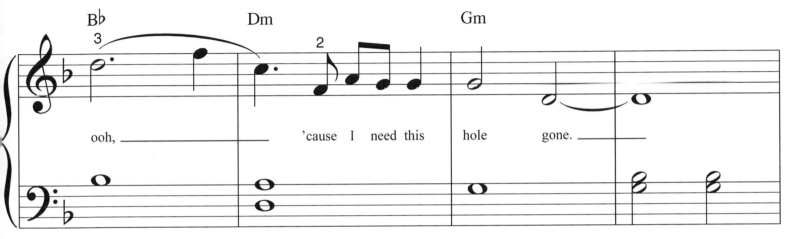

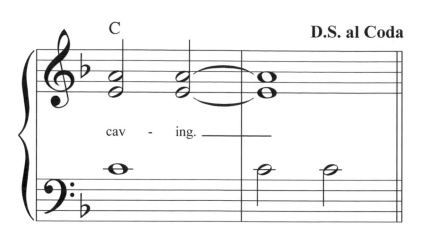

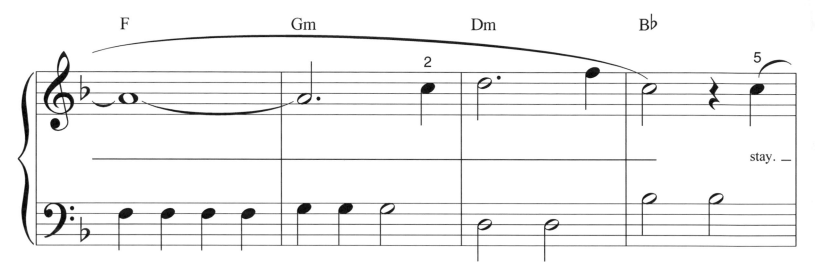

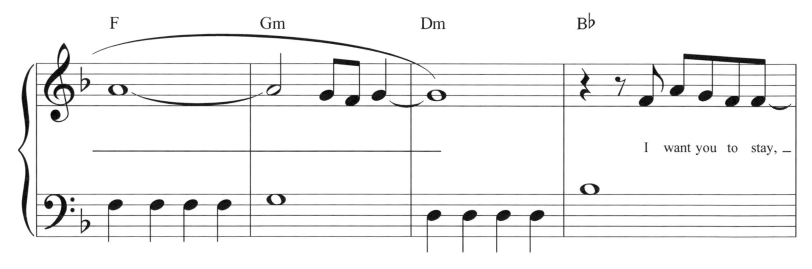

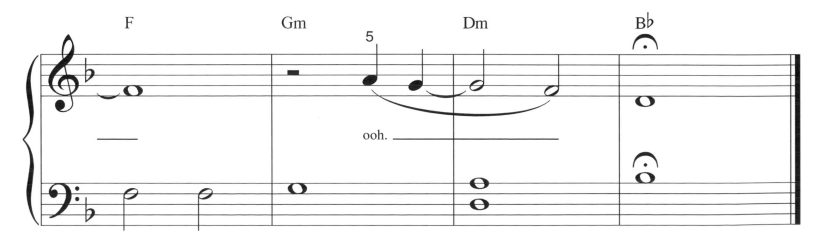

POMPEII

Words and Music by
DAN SMITH

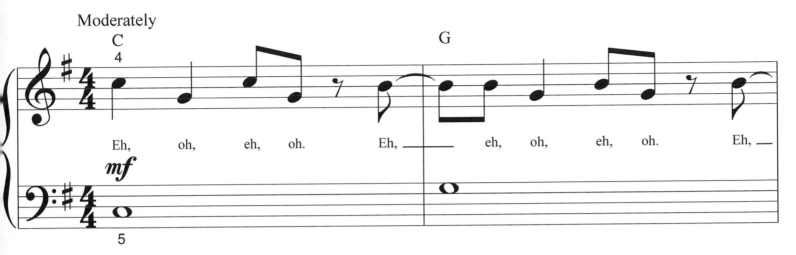

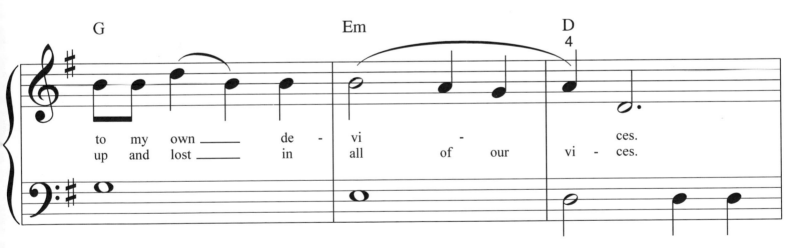

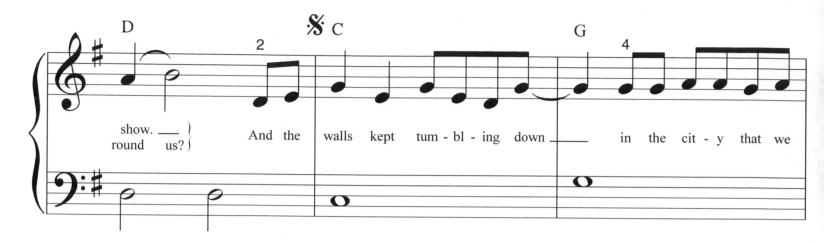

show. ———
round us?   And the walls kept tum-bl-ing down ——— in the cit-y that we

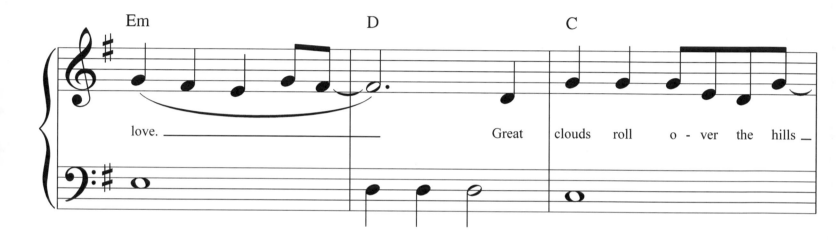

love. ——————   Great clouds roll o - ver the hills ——

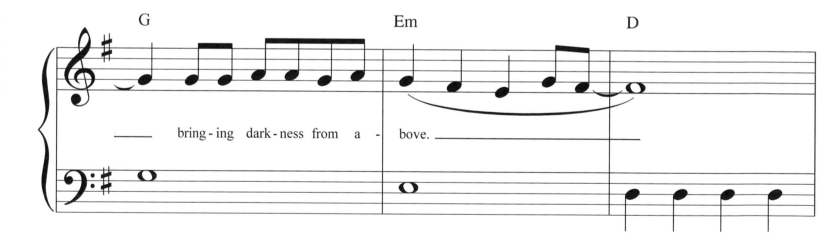

——— bring-ing dark-ness from a - bove. ———————

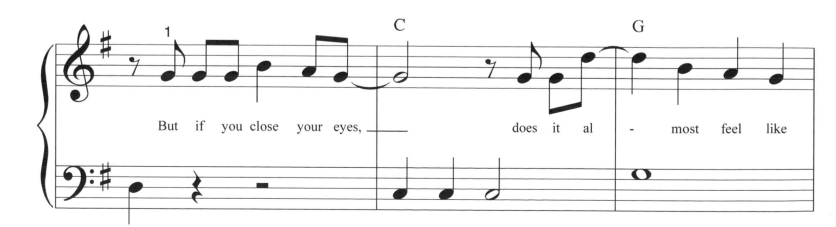

But if you close your eyes, ———   does it al - most feel like

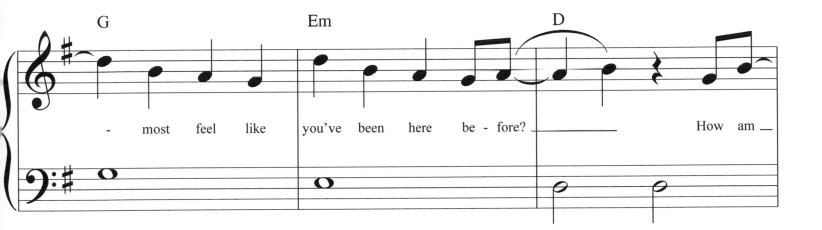

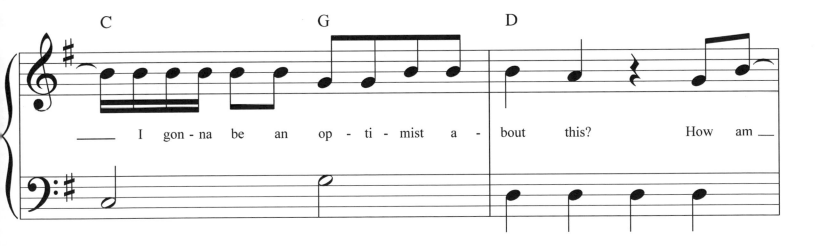

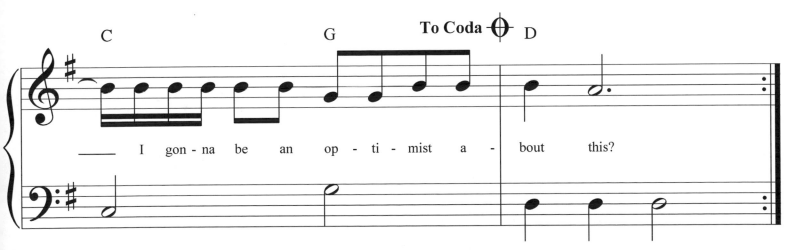

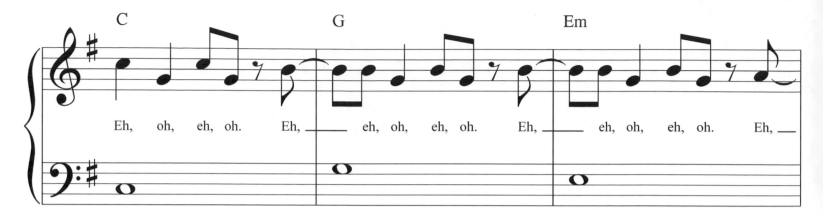

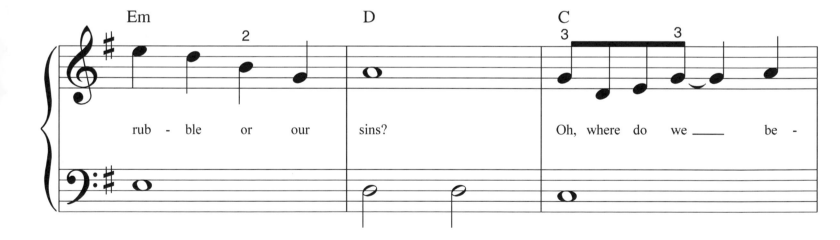

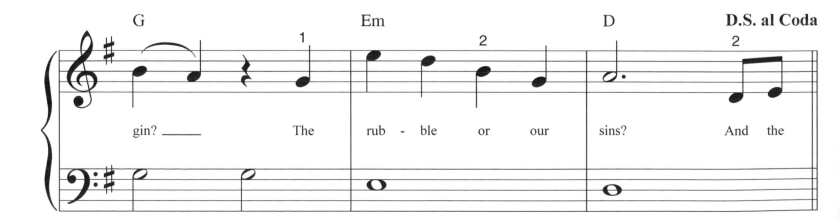

CODA

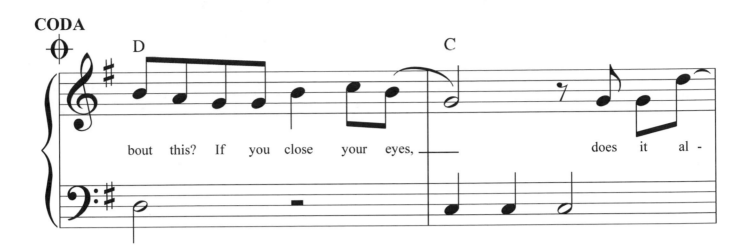

bout this? If you close your eyes, _____ does it al -

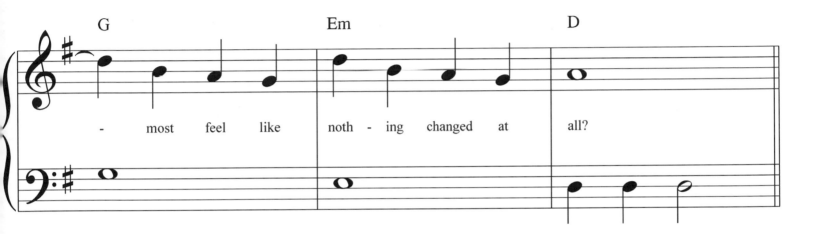

- most feel like noth - ing changed at all?

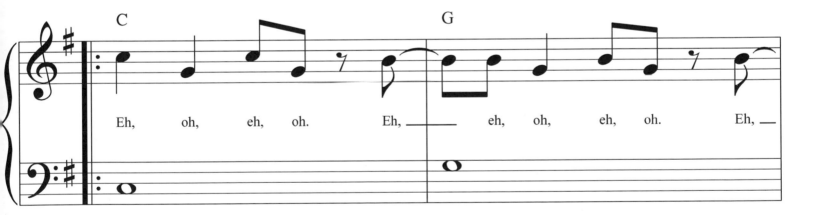

Eh, oh, eh, oh. Eh, ___ eh, oh, eh, oh. Eh, ___

___ eh, oh, eh, oh. Eh, ___ eh, oh, eh, oh.

RADIOACTIVE

Words and Music by DANIEL REYNOLDS,
BENJAMIN McKEE, DANIEL SERMON,
ALEXANDER GRANT and JOSH MOSSER

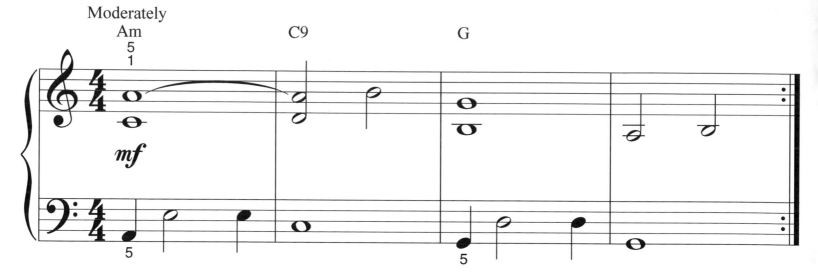

I'm wak - ing up to ash and dust; I wipe my
I raise my flag and dye my clothes. It's a rev - o -

brow and I sweat my rust. I'm breath - ing in the chem - i - cals.
lu - tion I sup - pose. We're paint - ed red to fit right in.

Whoa, _____ whoa. _____ I'm break - ing in _____

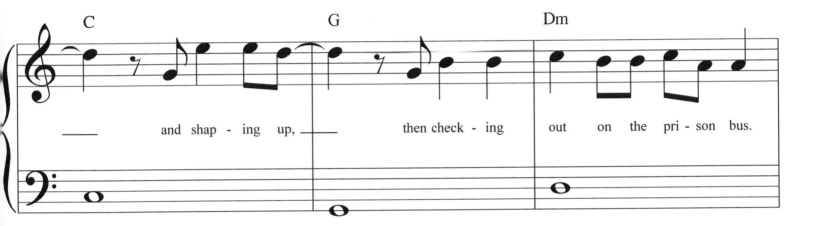

_____ and shap - ing up, _____ then check - ing out on the pri - son bus.

This is it, the A - poc - a - lypse. _____ Whoa. _____

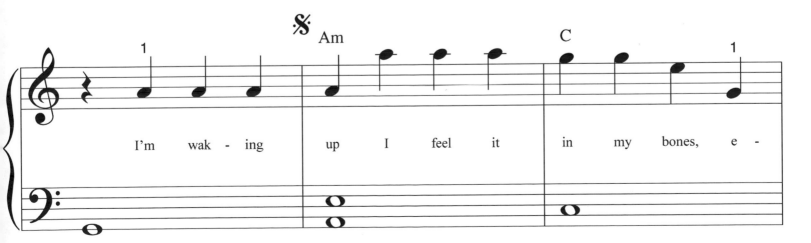

I'm wak - ing up I feel it in my bones, e -

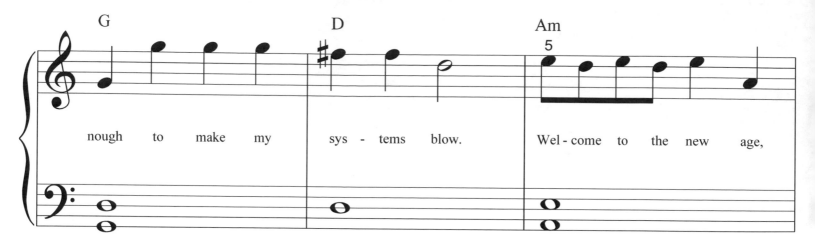

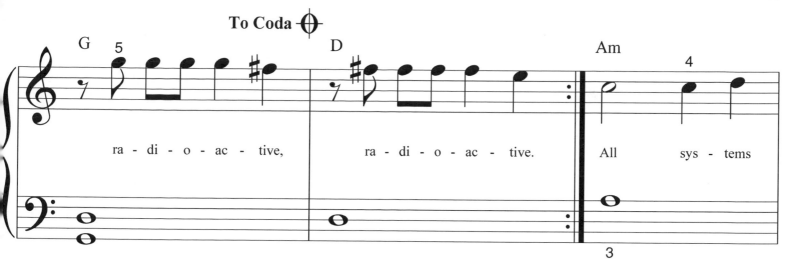

ra - di - o - ac - tive,   ra - di - o - ac - tive.   All   sys - tems

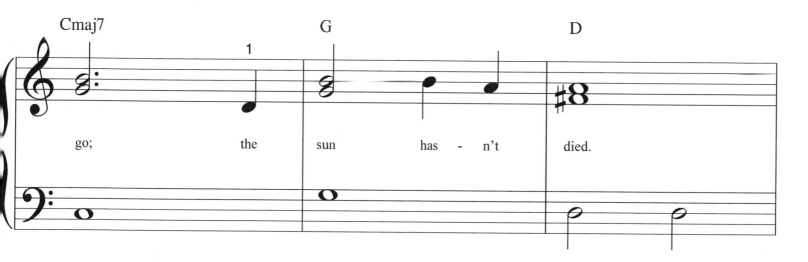

go;   the   sun   has - n't   died.

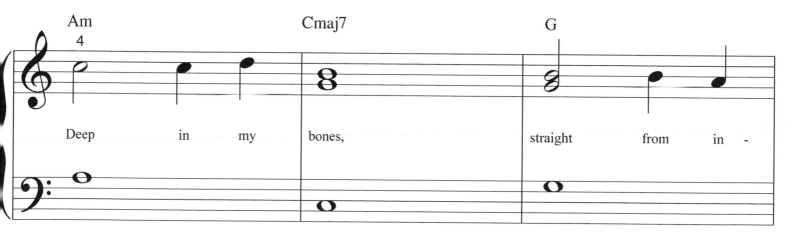

Deep   in my   bones,   straight   from   in -

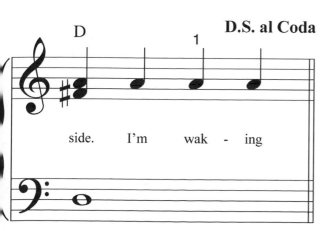

side. I'm wak - ing

ra - di - o - ac - tive.

ROAR

Words and Music by KATY PERRY,
LUKASZ GOTTWALD, MAX MARTIN,
BONNIE McKEE and HENRY WALTER

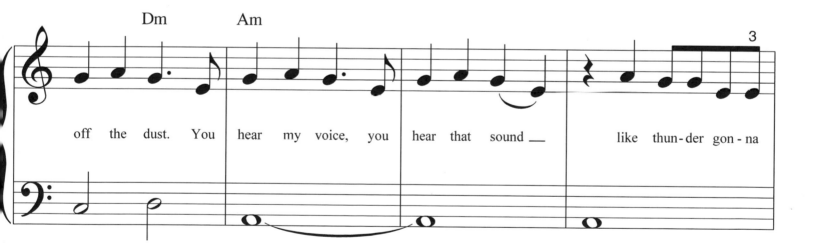

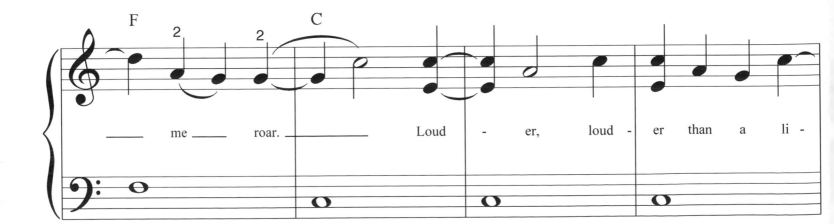

on 'cause I _____ am the cham - pion and you're gon - na hear ___

___ me ___ roar, _____ oh, ___

_____ oh. _____ You're gon - na hear ___

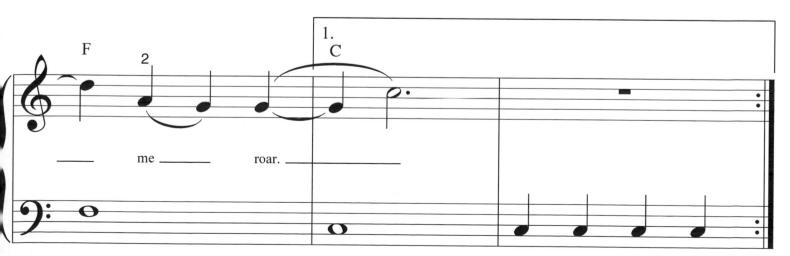

___ me ___ roar. ___

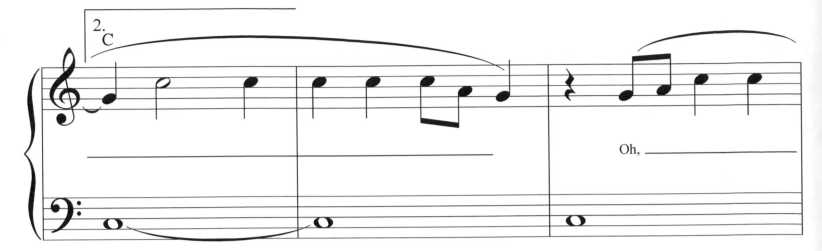

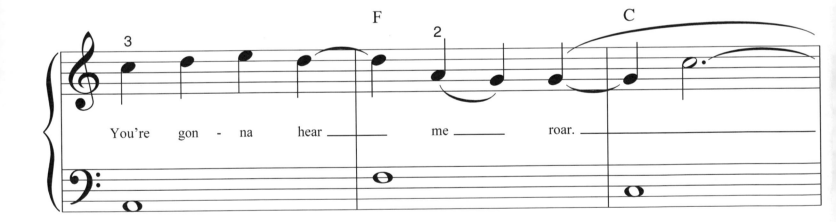

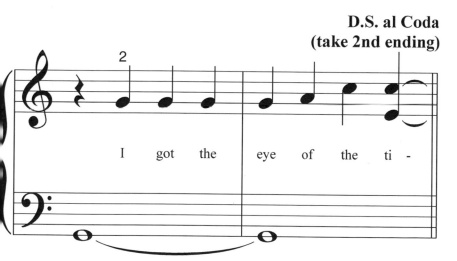

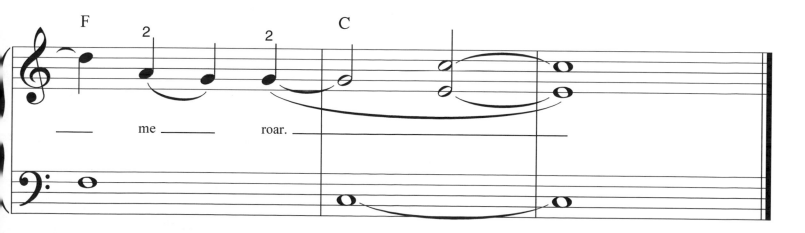

SEE YOU AGAIN
from FURIOUS 7

Words and Music by CAMERON THOMAZ,
CHARLIE PUTH, JUSTIN FRANKS
and ANDREW CEDAR

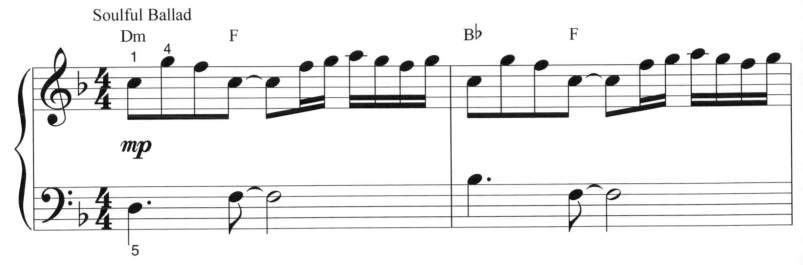

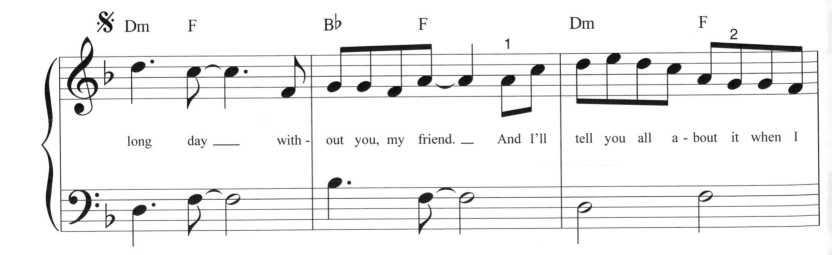

see you a - gain. ___ We've come a long way ___ from where we be - gan. ___ Oh, I'll

To Coda ⊕

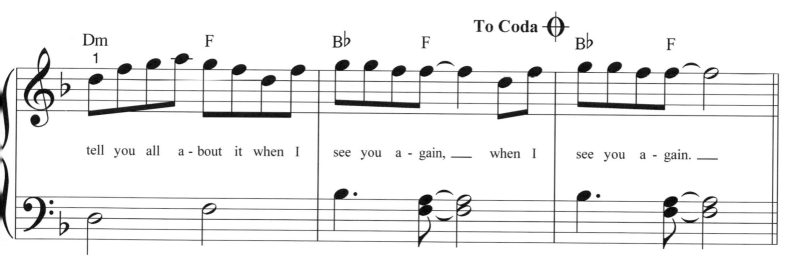

tell you all a - bout it when I see you a - gain, ___ when I see you a - gain. ___

Rap 1: *(See additional lyrics)*

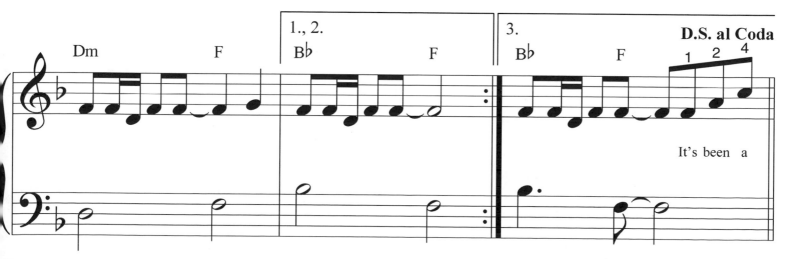

1., 2.

3.

D.S. al Coda

It's been a

see you a - gain. ___ Oh. ___ Oh. ___

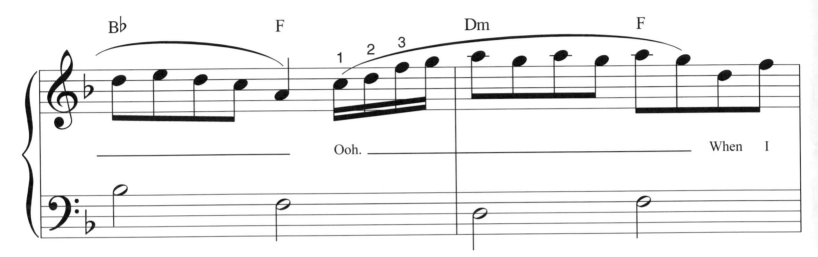

___ Ooh. ___ When I

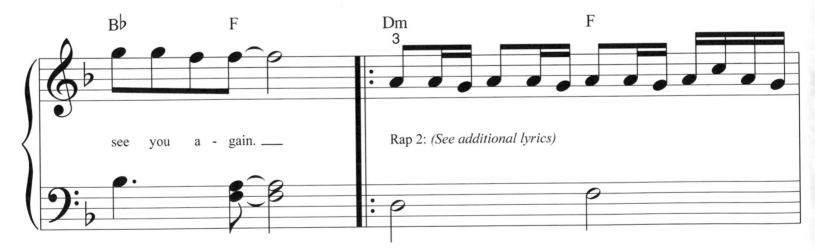

see you a - gain. ___ Rap 2: *(See additional lyrics)*

So let the light guide your

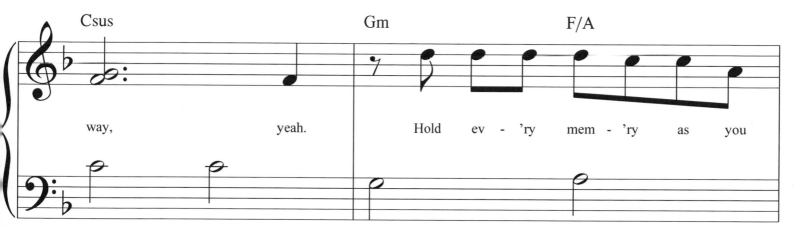

way, yeah. Hold ev - 'ry mem - 'ry as you

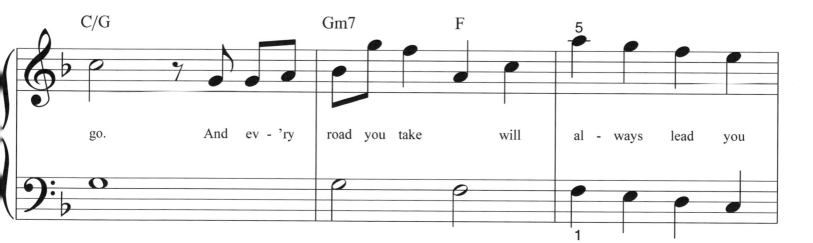

go. And ev - 'ry road you take will al - ways lead you

home, home. ___ It's been a long day ___ with -

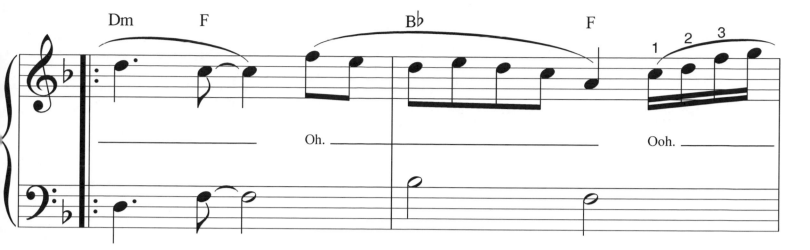

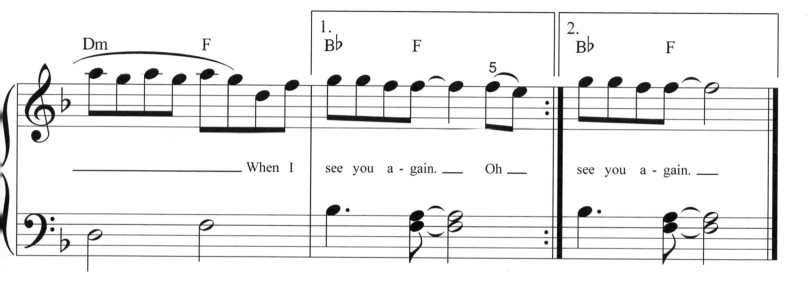

Additional Lyrics

Rap 1: Damn who knew all the planes we flew
Good things we've been through
That I'll be standing right here
Talking to you about another path I
Know we loved to hit the road and laugh
But something told me that it wouldn't last
Had to switch up look at things different see the bigger picture
Those were the days hard work forever pays now I see you in a better place

How could we not talk about family when family's all that we got?
Everything I went through you were standing there by my side
And now you gonna be with me for the last ride

Rap 2: First you both go out your way
And the vibe is feeling strong and what's
Small turn to a friendship, a friendship
Turn into a bond and that bond will never
Be broken and the love will never get lost
And when brotherhood come first then the line
Will never be crossed established it on our own
When that line had to be drawn and that line is what
We reach so remember me when I'm gone

How could we not talk about family when family's all that we got?
Everything I went through you were standing there by my side
And now you gonna be with me for the last ride

SHAKE IT OFF

Words and Music by TAYLOR SWIFT,
MAX MARTIN and SHELLBACK

at least, that's what peo - ple say, _____ mm, mm. That's what peo - ple
And that's what they don't know, _____ mm, mm. That's what they don't

Am

say, _____ mm, mm. But I keep cruis - ing;
know, _____ mm, mm. But I keep cruis - ing;

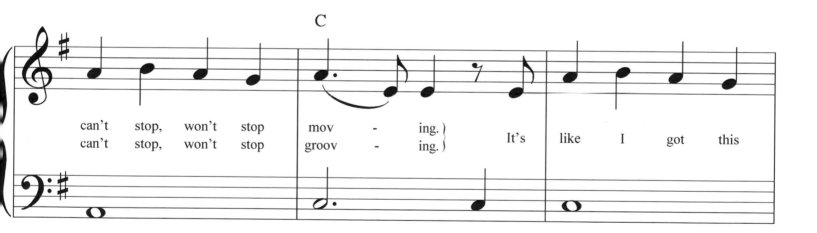

C

can't stop, won't stop mov - ing. It's like I got this
can't stop, won't stop groov - ing. It's like I got this

G

mu - sic in my mind say - ing, "It's gon - na be al -

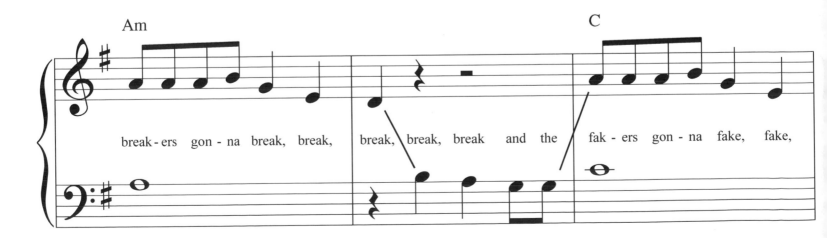

fake, fake, fake, ba - by. I'm just gon - na shake, shake, shake, shake, shake; — I

To Coda 1.

shake it off, I shake it off. I nev - er miss a

2.

off. I

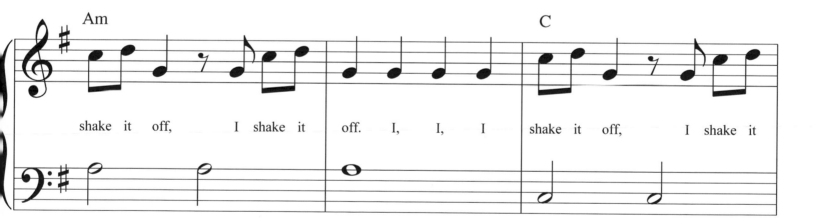

Am

shake it off, I shake it off. I, I, I

C

shake it off, I shake it

G

off. I, I, I shake it off, I shake it off. I, I, I

N.C.

shake it off,   I shake it   off. (Ooh, __ ooh!)

1. *Spoken: (See additional lyrics)*
2. Rap: *(See additional lyrics)*

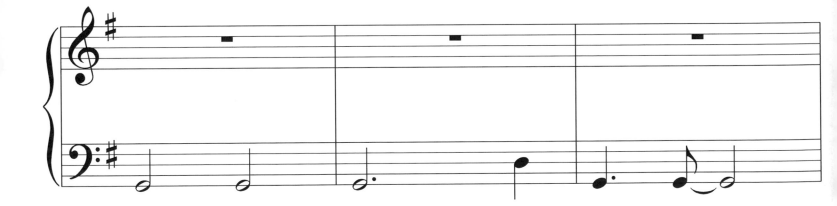

D.S. al Coda

Rap ends   Yeah,   oh. _____ 'Cause the

CODA

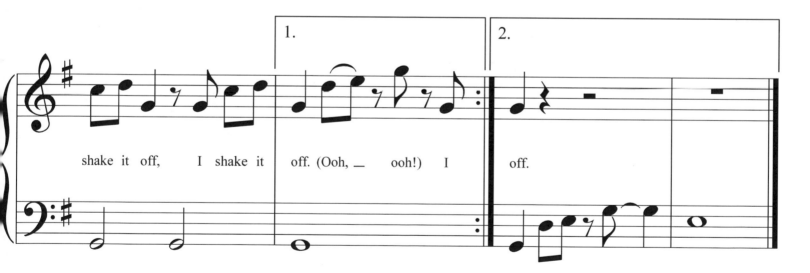

Additional Lyrics

*Spoken: Hey, hey, hey! Just think: While you've been getting
Down and out about the liars and the dirty, dirty
Cheats of the world, you could've been getting down to
This. Sick. Beat!*

Rap: My ex-man brought his new girlfriend.
She's like, "Oh, my god!" But I'm just gonna shake.
And to the fella over there with the hella good hair,
Won't you come on over, baby? We can shake, shake, shake.

A SKY FULL OF STARS

Words and Music by GUY BERRYMAN,
JON BUCKLAND, WILL CHAMPION,
CHRIS MARTIN and TIM BERGLING

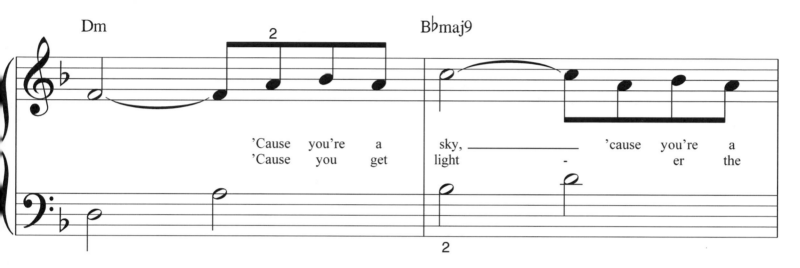

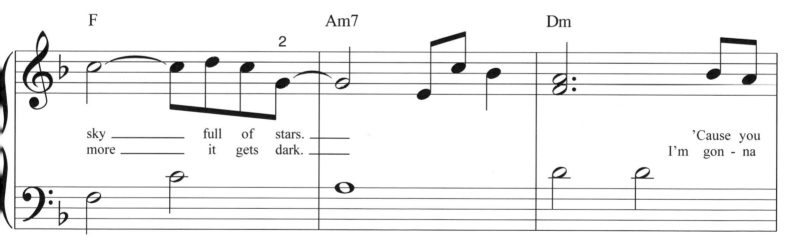

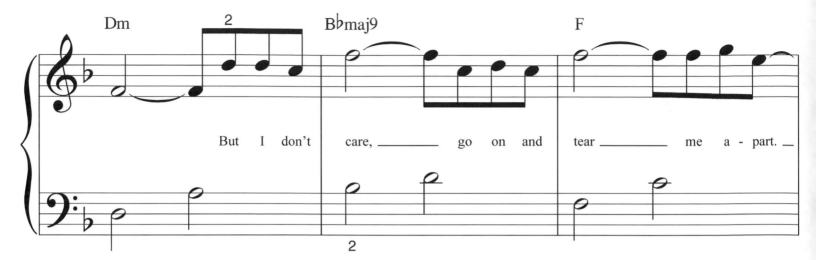

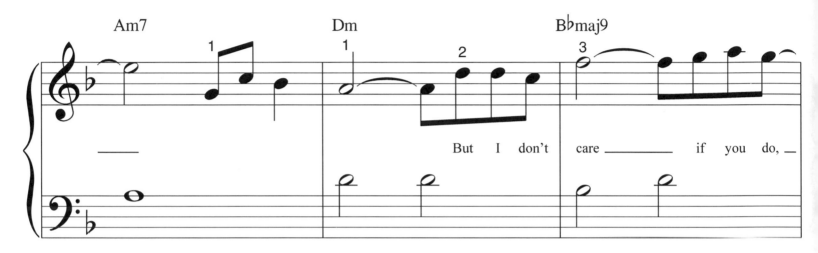

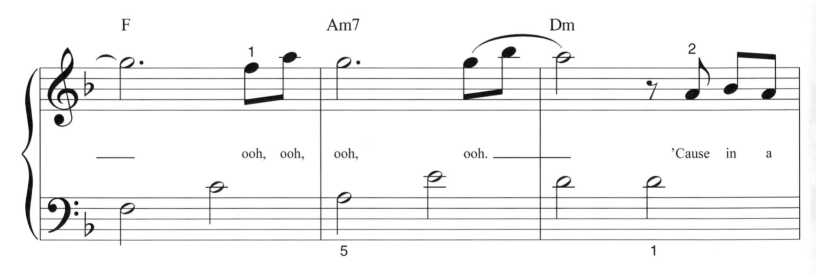

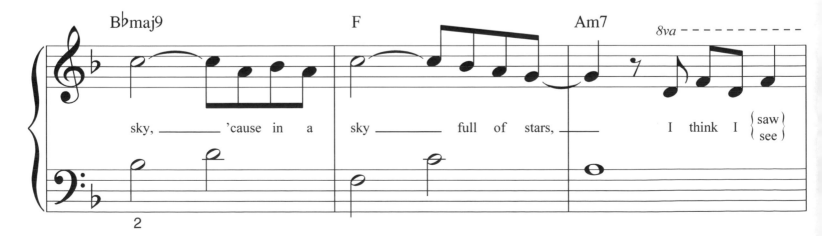

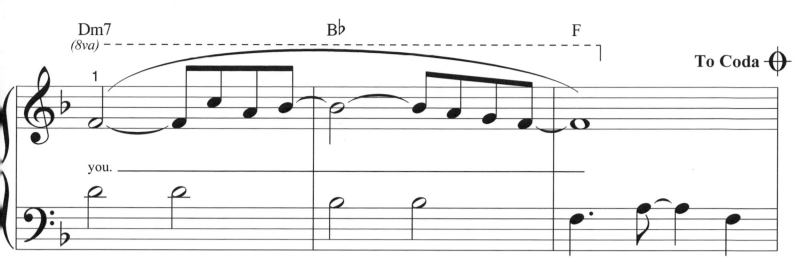

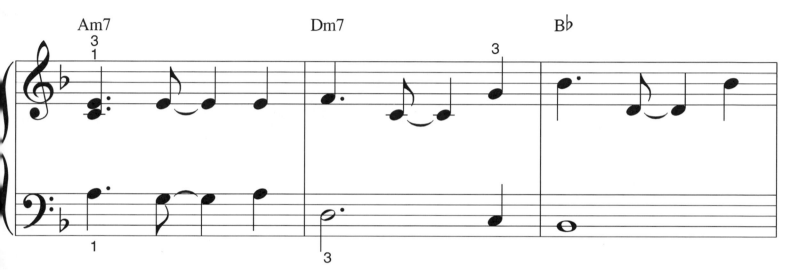

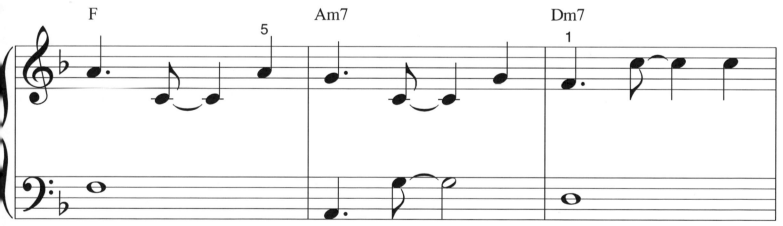

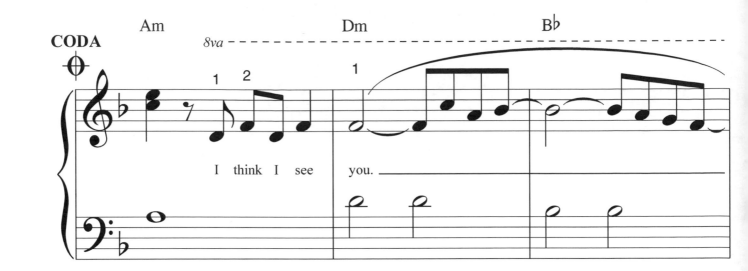

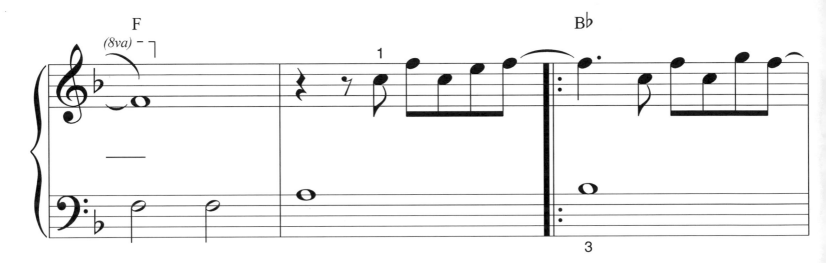

I think I see you.

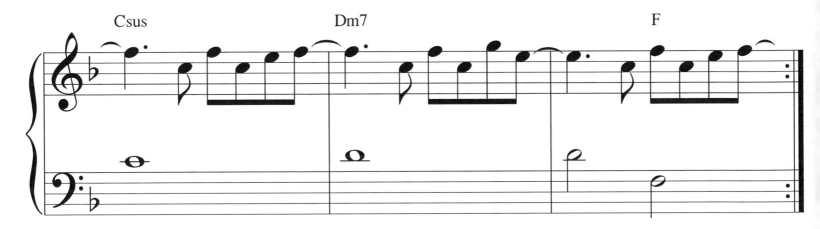

'Cause you're a sky, _____ you're a sky _____ full of stars, _____

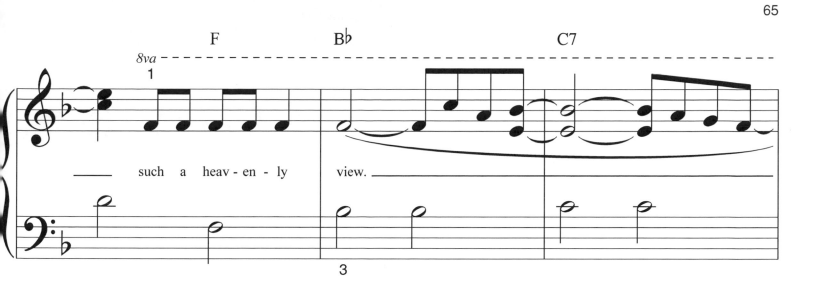

such a heav - en - ly view.

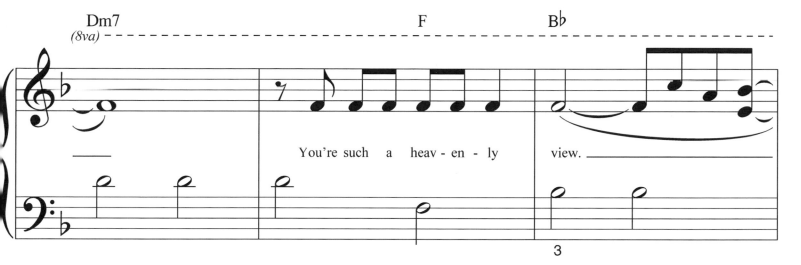

You're such a heav - en - ly view.

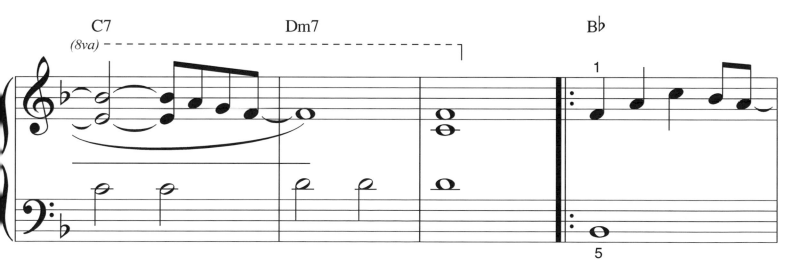

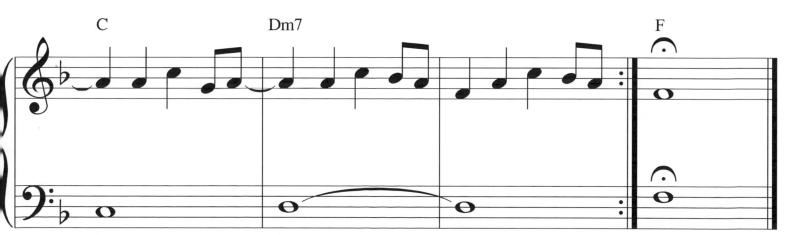

STORY OF MY LIFE

Words and Music by JAMIE SCOTT,
JOHN HENRY RYAN, JULIAN BUNETTA,
HARRY STYLES, LIAM PAYNE,
LOUIS TOMLINSON, NIALL HORAN
and ZAIN MALIK

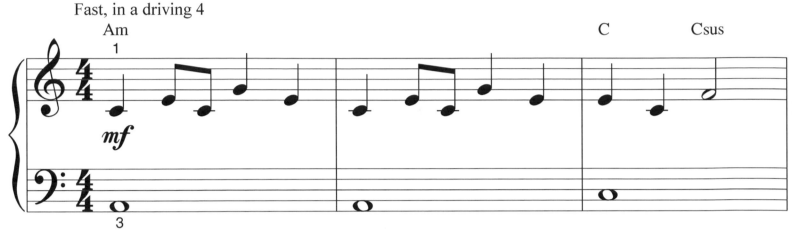

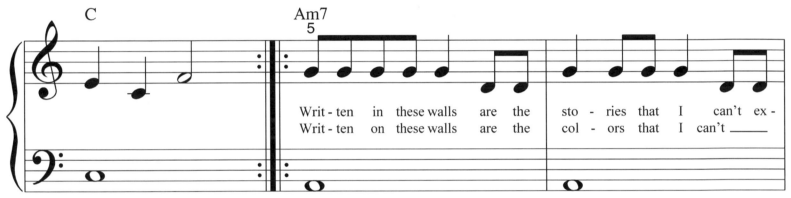

Writ - ten in these walls are the sto - ries that I can't ex -
Writ - ten on these walls are the col - ors that I can't

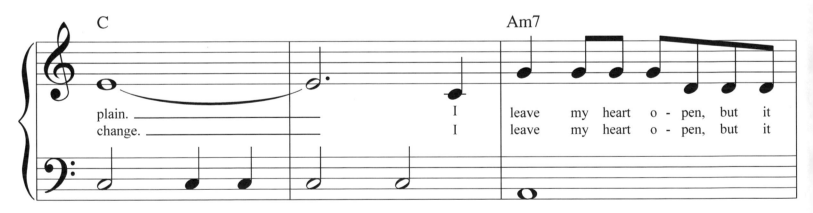

plain. ___ I
change. ___ I

leave my heart o - pen, but it
leave my heart o - pen, but it

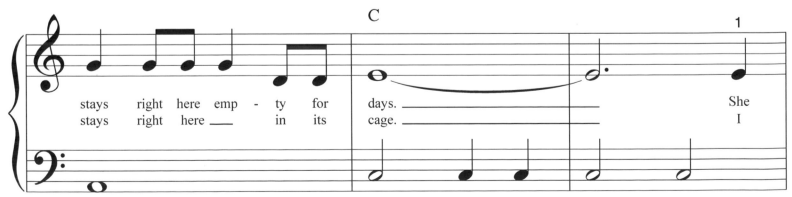

stays right here emp - ty for days. ___ She
stays right here ___ in its cage. ___ I

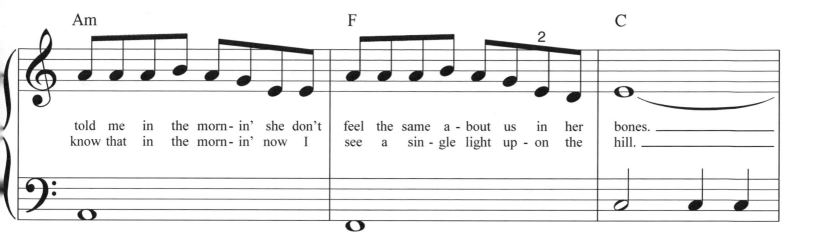

told me in the mornin' she don't
know that in the mornin' now I

feel the same a-bout us in her
see a sin-gle light up-on the

bones. _____
hill. _____

_____
_____ Al - though

Seems to me that when I die, these
I am bro - ken, my

words will be writ-ten on my
heart is un - tamed _____ still. _

stone. _____

And I'll be gone, gone to - night. _
And I'll be gone, gone to - night. _

_____ The ground be - neath my
_____ The fire be - neath my

feet is o - pen wide, _____
feet is burn - in' bright, _____

the way that I've been
the way that I've been

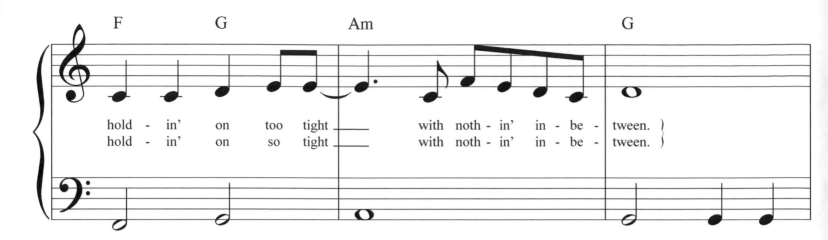

hold - in'   on   too tight ____   with noth - in'   in - be - tween.
hold - in'   on   so tight ____   with noth - in'   in - be - tween.

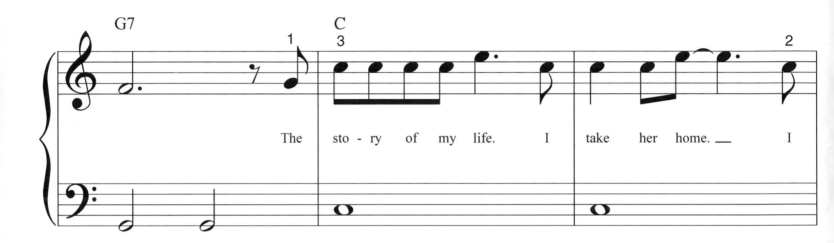

The   sto - ry   of   my   life.   I   take   her   home. ___   I

drive   all   night ___   to   keep   her   warm ___   and   time _____   is

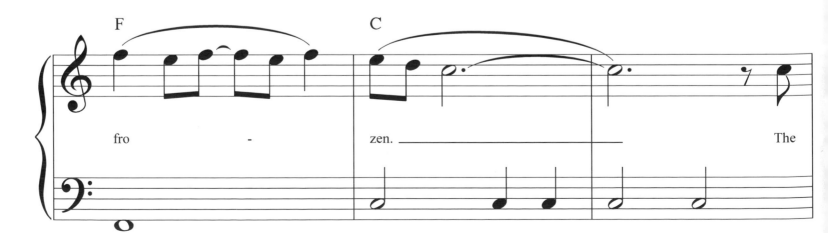

fro - zen. _____   The

69

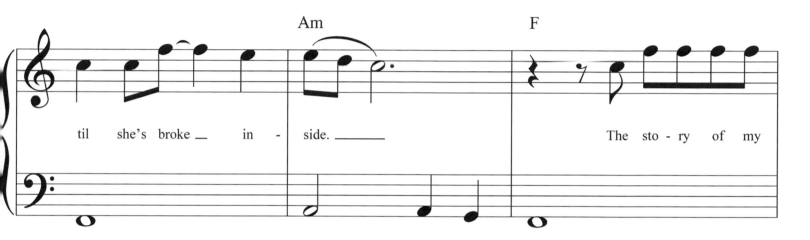

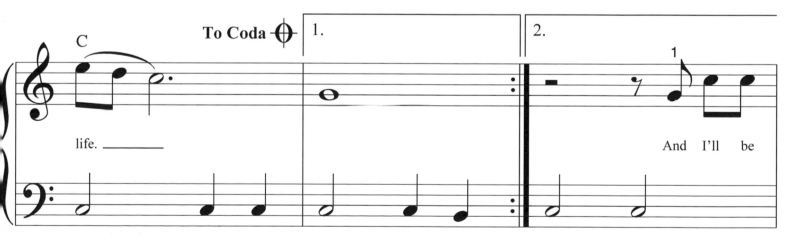

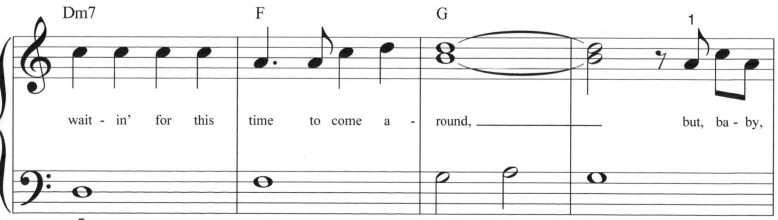

run - in' af - ter you is like chas - in' the clouds. ___

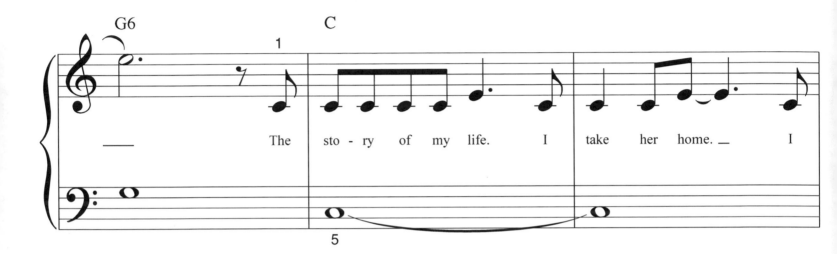

___ The sto - ry of my life. I take her home. ___ I

drive all night ___ to keep her warm. ___ And time ___ is

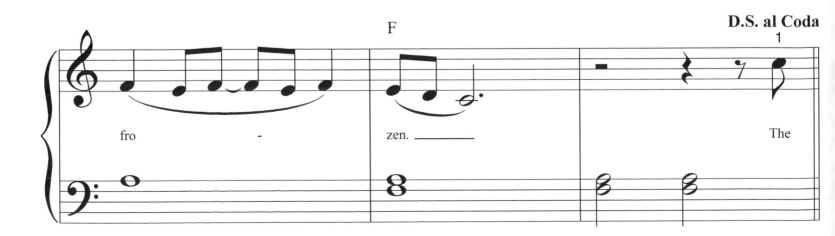

fro - zen. ___ The

D.S. al Coda

CODA

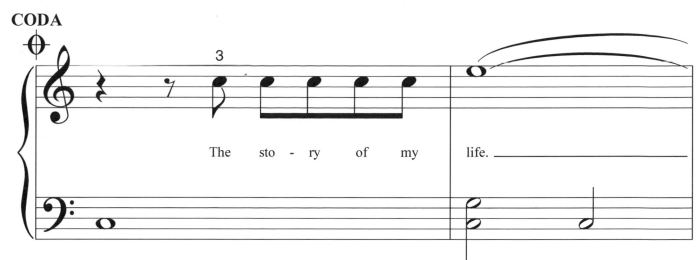

The sto - ry of my life. _____

F

The sto - ry of my

Am   F

life. _____

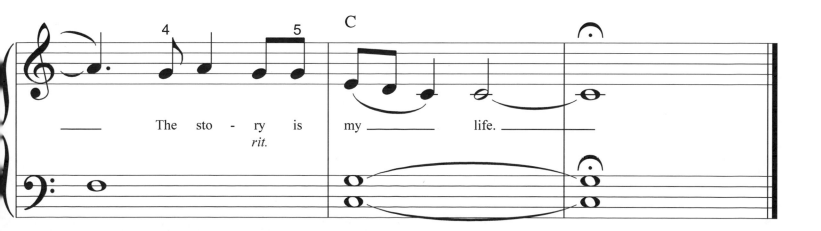

The sto - ry is my _____ life. _____

rit.

THINKING OUT LOUD

Words and Music by ED SHEERAN
and AMY WADGE

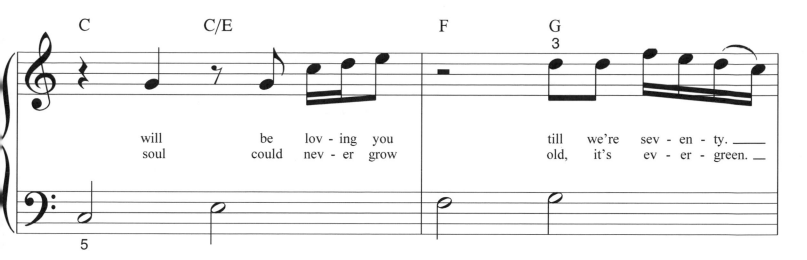

will be lov - ing you till we're sev - en - ty. ____
soul could nev - er grow old, it's ev - er - green. __

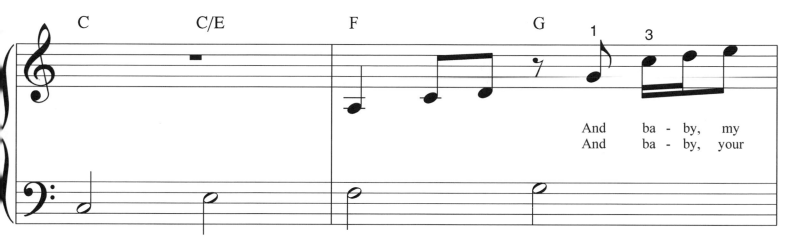

And ba - by, my
And ba - by, your

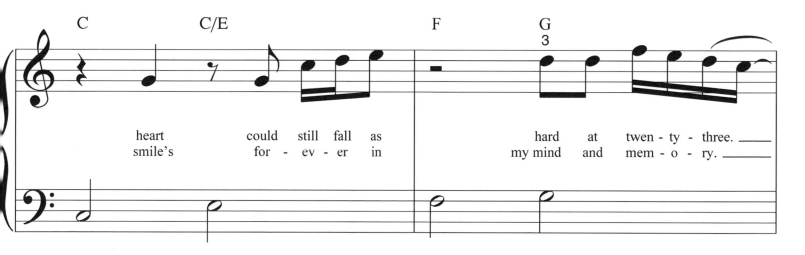

heart could still fall as hard at twen - ty - three. ____
smile's for - ev - er in my mind and mem - o - ry. ____

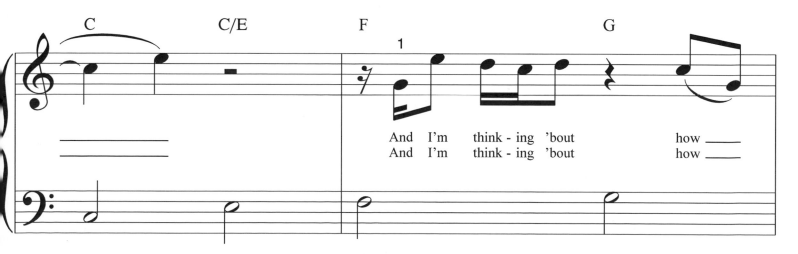

And I'm think - ing 'bout how ____
And I'm think - ing 'bout how ____

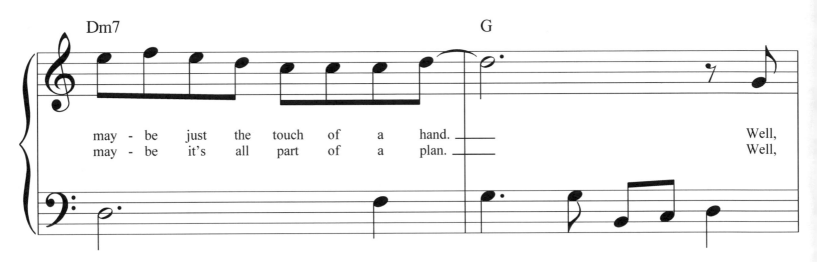

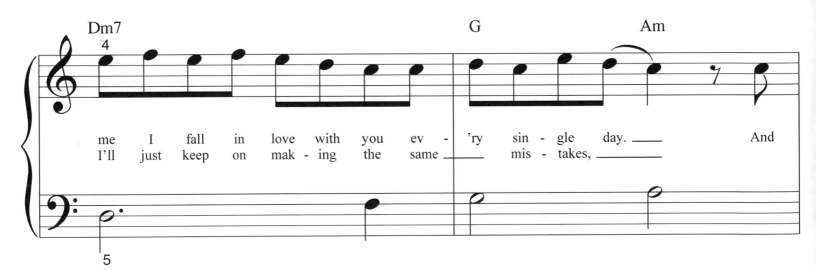

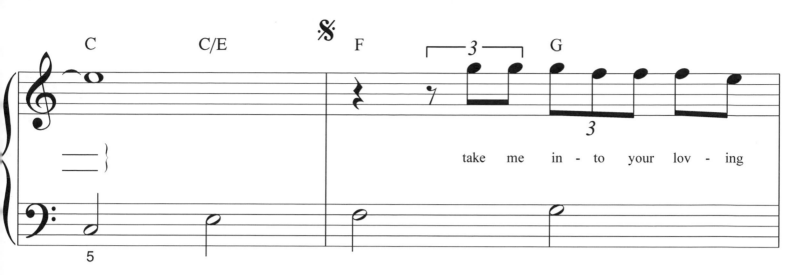

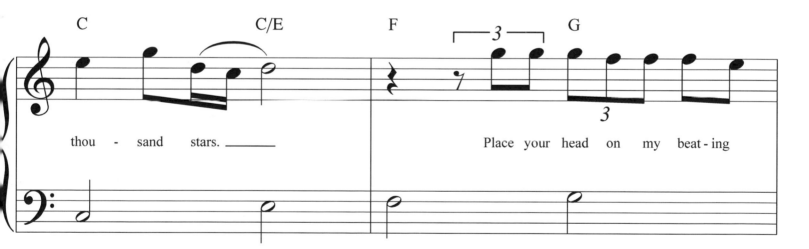

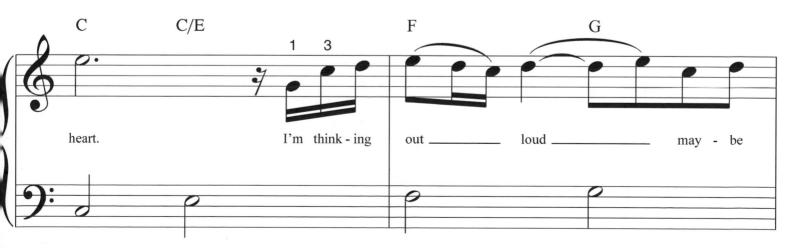

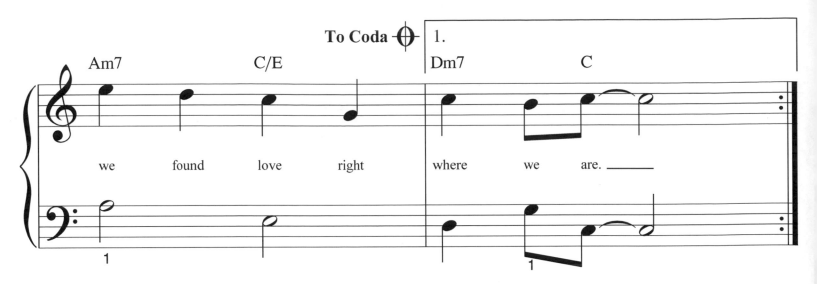

To Coda ⊕ 1.

Am7   C/E   Dm7   C

we found love right where we are. _____

2.

Dm7   C

where we are.   *Instrumental solo*

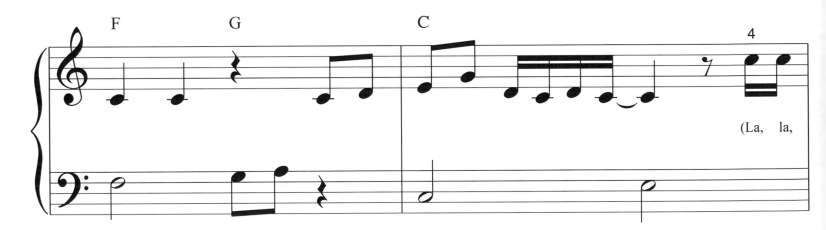

F   G   C

(La, la,

F   G   C

la, la, la, la, la, la, la, la, la, la.)

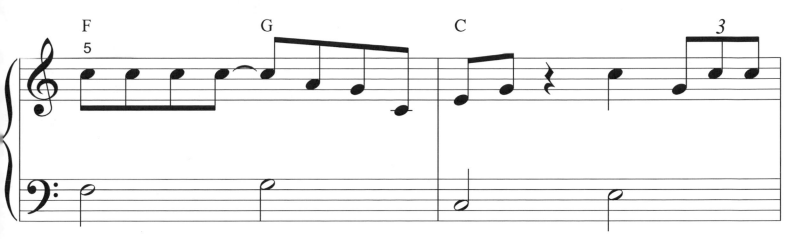

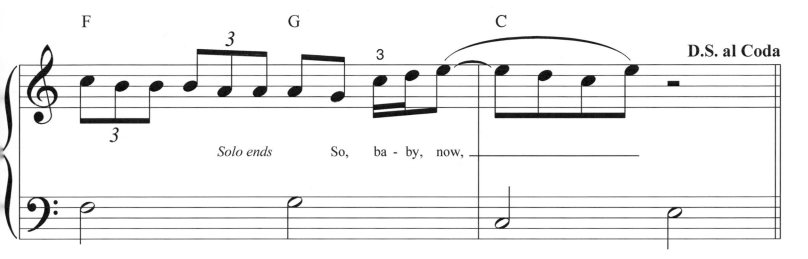

Solo ends   So, ba - by, now, ____

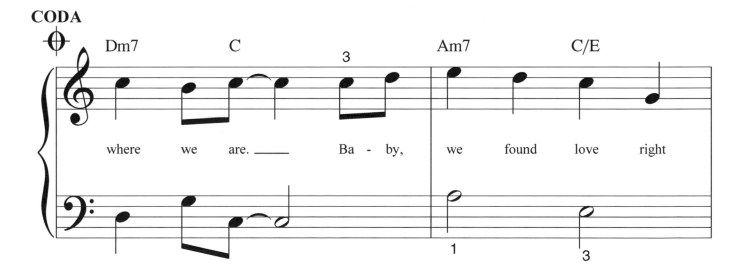

where   we   are. ____   Ba - by,   we   found   love   right

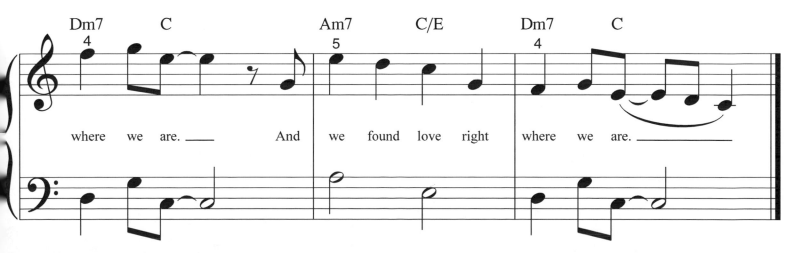

where   we   are. ____   And   we   found   love   right   where   we   are. ____

STAY WITH ME

Words and Music by SAM SMITH,
JAMES NAPIER, WILLIAM EDWARD PHILLIPS,
TOM PETTY and JEFF LYNNE

Moderate Soul

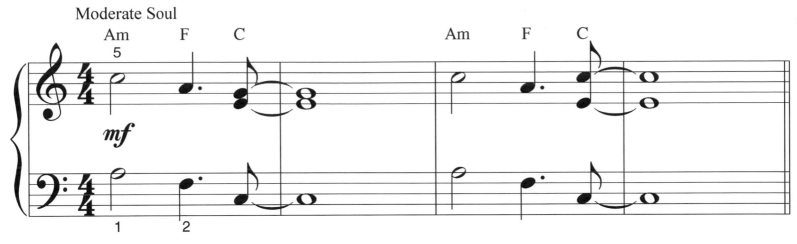

Guess it's true, I'm not good at a one-night stand.
Why am I so e-mo-tion-al?

But I still need love 'cause I'm just a man.
No, it's not a good look. Gain some self con-trol.

These nights nev-er seem to go to plan.
And deep down I ____ know this nev-er works.

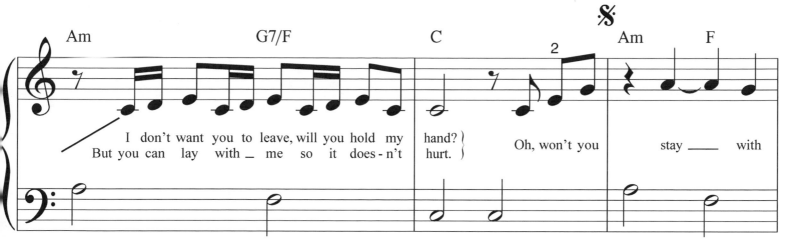

I don't want you to leave, will you hold my hand?
But you can lay with me so it does-n't hurt.
Oh, won't you stay _____ with

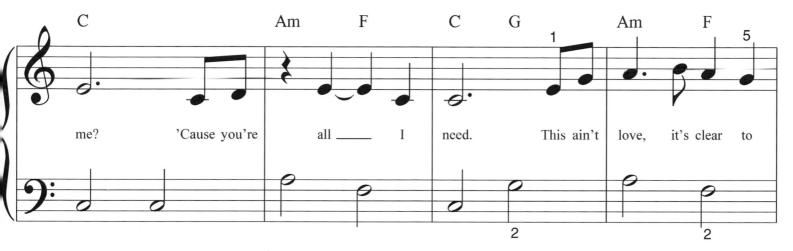

me? 'Cause you're all _____ I need. This ain't love, it's clear to

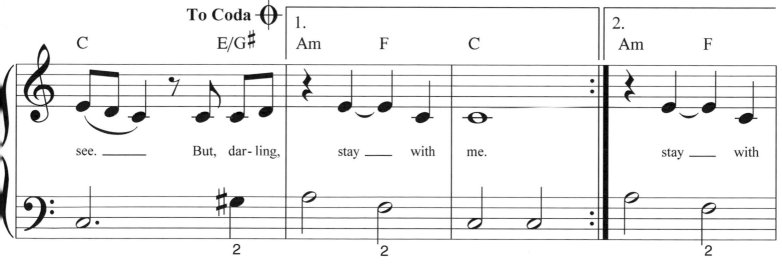

see. _____ But, dar-ling, stay _____ with me. stay _____ with

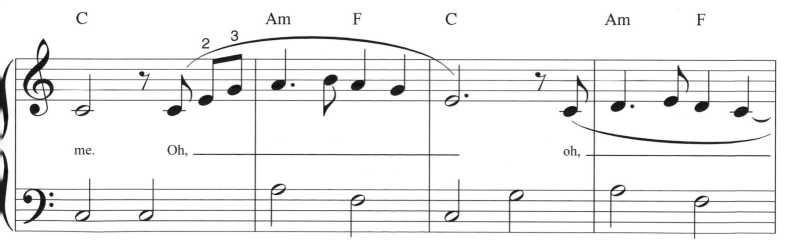

me. Oh, _____ oh, _____

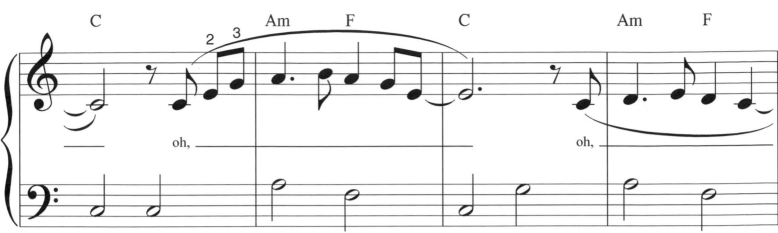

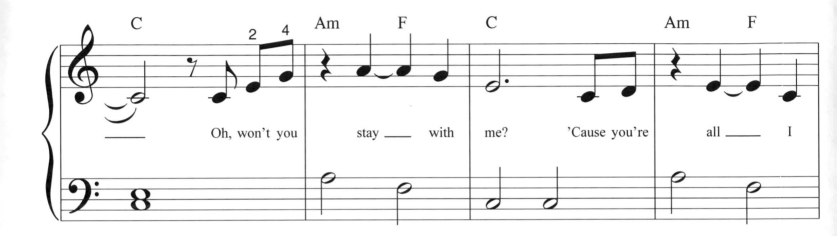

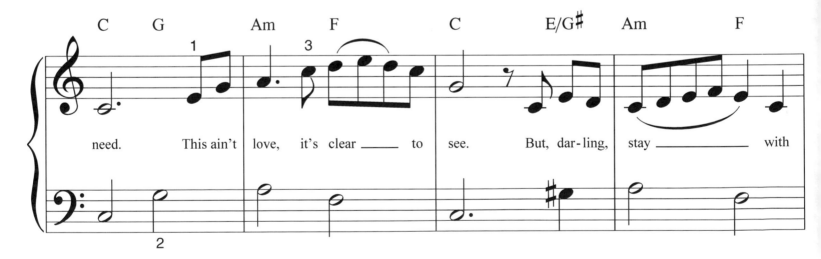

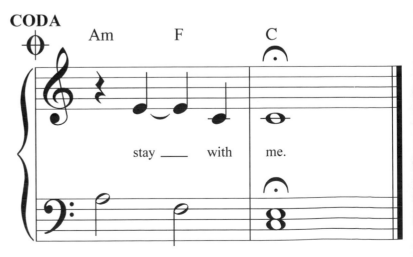